Son Of Perfection, Part 2

Hilton Hotema

SON OF PERFECTION

(In Two Parts)

PART TWO

by

Prof. Hilton Hotema

A Summary of the Hidden Teachings of the Apocalypse

By Chapter and Verse

The Revelation of Saint John The Divine

From the Original Greek, with an interpretation of the
Symbols and Parables, based on--

THE LOST WISDOM OF THE ANCIENT MASTERS

***   ***   ***

Chapter	Title	Chapter	Title
13.	Active Kundalini	27.	John Chapter 13
14.	The Drama	28.	John Chapter 14
15.	The Apocalypse	29.	John Chapter 15
16.	John Chapter 2	30.	John Chapter 16
17.	John Chapter 3	31.	John Chapter 17
18.	John Chapter 4	32.	John Chapter 18
19.	John Chapter 5	33.	John Chapter 19
20.	John Chapter 6	34.	John Chapter 20
21.	John Chapter 7	35.	John Chapter 21
22.	John Chapter 8	36.	John Chapter 22
23.	John Chapter 9	37.	Analysis of Apocalypse
24.	John Chapter 10	38.	Explanatory Statements
25.	John Chapter 11	39.	Seven Grades of Being
26.	John Chapter 12	40.	The Cosmic Cycle

CHAPTER NO. 13

The Active Kundalini

In activating the Kundalini by conscious effort in meditation, the Sushumna, while it is the all-important force, is ignored; and the mind is centered on the Ida and Pingala. For the Sushumna cannot be energized alone, and it does not start into action until the two side-currents have preceded it, forming a positive and negative current along the spinal cord.

The Ida and Pingala currents, on reaching the Ajna chakra at the Pituitary, radiate to right and left, along the line of the eyebrows. Then the Sushumna current, starting at the Muladhara chakra, flows up thru the Sushumna, its passage thru each chakra producing a violent shock, or rushing sensation, due to the accession of force, until it reaches the Pineal, and thence passes outward thru the Brahmarandhra, which means "the hole of Brahms," or the soft spot in the crown of a baby's head. This is also termed the home of Silva by the Hindus and depicted in their literature as a serpent protruding from the top of the head (p. 44).

In the initial stage, the seven psychic colors are seen; and when the Sushumna current impinges upon the Pineal gland, there follows the lofty consciousness of the Seer, whose Single Eye (Pineal) now becomes, as it has been poetically expressed, "a window into space." In the Bible, it is termed "a door opened in heaven." (Rev. 4:1).

In the next stage, as the brain-centers are successively "raised from the dead" by the solar force, the seven "psychic sounds" are heard in the tense and vibrant aura of the Seer; and in the Bible it is termed "like a trumpet-call speaking to me." (Rev. 4:1).

In the succeeding stage, seeing and hearing become blended into one sense, by which colors are heard and sounds are seen; or, more correctly speaking, color and sound blend and become one and are perceived by a sense that is neither seeing nor hearing, but both. Concerning this phenomenon, the Bible says, "Come up hither, and I will show thee things which must be hereafter." (Rev. 4:1).

As clear light contains all the colors of the rainbow, so cosmic vibrations contain all the qualities of sensation, the various differences being filtered out of the vibrations by the various sense organs of the body. But of course this is impossible if the sense organs are dormant, as in the case of the deaf or blind man.

When the solar electricity has activated the Pituitary and Pineal glands, sight and hearing blend into a single sense, as stated, by which colors and sounds are both seen and heard.

That is the function of the sixth and seventh sense powers which overcome the time-space element; and so Apollonius, while preaching in Ephesus, saw the assassination of the tyrant Domitian in Rome, many miles away, as we explained in The Mystery Man of the Bible (p. 18). ($4.50 from HEALTH RESEARCH.)

We do not have to see the source of sound to hear the sound; and with the sixth and seventh sense powers active, man can see all objects that emit vibrations which contact his eyes, no matter where located.

So, the assassination of the Roman tyrant miles away was such a startling event that it produced vibrations in the ether so strong that they contracted the sixth and seventh sense powers of Apollonius.

We can hear any sound whose vibrations contact our ear drums, but the deaf man hears nothing because his ear drums are dormant.

So the Seer can see any event that emits vibrations which contact his ears--eyes, regardless of distance; whereas the common man cannot because his sixth and seventh sense powers are dormant.

This is the scientific explanation of the "uncanny" powers of the wild Indians of South America, as mentioned in THE KINGDOM OF HEAVEN, page 19. (by Hotema - $3.50 from HEALTH RESEARCH.)

Also, the psychic senses of taste and smell become unified; and next the two senses, thus reduced from four, are merged in the interior, intimate sense of touch, which in turn vanishes into the epistemonic faculty, the gnostic power of the Seer, exalted above all sense perceptions, to cognize eternal realities.

This is the sacred trance called Samadhi in Sanscrit and Manteia in Greek. In the ancient literature of both of these languages, four such trances are mentioned.

It is said that these stages of seership are but the beginning of the telestic labor, the culmination of which is "Rebirth in the imperishable solar body."

We are not quite sure as to the correct interpretation of this statement. The Solar Body is the imperishable Man, without beginning and without end, who is never born and never dies, as stated in that very ancient Hindu work, the "Bhagavad Gita," in these words:

"Unborn, undying ancient, perpetual and eternal, it (Solar Man) hath endured and will endure forever." (p. 27).

But the Apocalypse has for its sole theme this "spiritual rebirth," and we must recognize that doctrine in our interpretation of its symbols and parables.

The Apocalypse is a coherent whole, symmetrical, with every detail fitted into its appropriate place with great care.

In orderly arrangement and concise statement, the book is a model of precise literary workmanship. It contains a series of puzzles, some based upon the numerical values of certain Greek words, thereby serving to verify the correct interpretation of the more important symbols. As the detailed explanation of these in the analysis would interrupt the interpretation of the work as a whole, for the sake of clearness, the solution of these puzzles will here be noticed in advance.

First, four animal-symbols or beasts are conspicuous dramatis personae:

1. A Lamb, having seven horns and seven eyes, identified as Iesous (Solar Man) who becomes "the Conqueror." This is the candidate to be initiated.

2. A beast resembling a Leopard, with a bear's feet and a lion's mouth, having seven heads and ten horns. This represents the lower mind.

3. A red Dragon, having seven heads and ten horns. This represents Desire.

4. A beast having two horns like a Lamb, but speaking like a Dragon, and who is called the Pseudo-Seer, or false teacher. This represents Sensuality.

Of these four, the Leopard is particularly referred to as "the Beast;" and concerning it the Apocalyptist says:

"Here is the cleverness (sphia); he who has the Nous, let him count the number of the Beast; for it is the number of man, and his number is 666."

The words "The Nous," the term in Greek philosophy for the higher mind, or man, suggests the correct answer, he phren, the cognate term for the lower mind, or man.

As numbers are expressed in Greek by the letters of the alphabet, and not by arithmetical figures, the number of a name is simply the sum of the numerical values of the letters composing it. Thus the numerical value of "he phren" is 666.

It will be noticed that the Beast, the phrenic mind, is the faculty ruling over one of the four divisions of the body, from which it is natural to infer that the three other beasts likewise are the regents of the other three.

The Lamb, Iesous, would stand for the highest of these, the Nous. The word Iesous gives the sum 888.

The red Dragon, "the archaic serpent" fits neatly into place as the ruler of the third division of the body, epithumia, which word yields the number 555.

The fourth beast, the "False Prophet," takes his place in the fourth division as the generative principle, akrasia (sensuality), the number of his name being 333.

Placing these four names, with their numbers, in the form of a diagram of the four divisions of the body, we note that the puzzle is still only partly solved, as a complete series of numbers is intended.

A space is left where the diagram, to complete the meaning requires the Cross and another space for the "good serpent," the regenerative force; the "bad serpent" (Dragon) the desire that leads to animalistic generation, being already included. The number of the Cross (stauros) is 777.

The spiraling electric force (Kundalini) is the Speirema, which words gives the number 444.

The effect of this force upon the brain, where its triple current forms the cross, gives the noetic perception, direct cognition (the episteme, or highest degree of knowledge as defined by Plato), and to express this in the diagram, it becomes necessary to insert the word "epistemon;" its numerical value is 999.

He who has reached this higher knowledge becomes the Conqueror and, as "The Conqueror" is the hero of the Apocalyptic Drama, his name must be placed at the head of the list, as "ho nikon," with its number 1,000.

The diagram thus completed reveals the basic teaching of the Apocalypse, which treats of the Kundalini and its energizing thru the chakras, as the Conqueror gains mastery over them and builds up his immortal vehicle, the monogenetic or solar body.

This deathless solar vesture is symbolized as a city that comes down out of the sky, enveloped in the radiance of the Solar God. The description, with its wealth of detail, should be sufficient to show clearly what the city is; but Apollonius has supplied conclusive proof of the true meaning by inserting in the description a puzzle which reads as follows:

"The Divinity who was talking with me has for a measure a golden reed, to measure the city, its gateways, and its wall. The city lies foursquare, and its length is as great as the width.

"He measured the city with the reed, by stadia, twelve thousand; its length, width, and height are equal. And he measured its wall, one hundred forty-four cubits (including) the measure of a man, that is, of a Divinity."

In a few words, what we have here is a cube; and when the cube is unfolded, it forms a Cross, the figure of a man, standing erect with feet together and arms extended as right angles. The Cross is a cubical city unfolded, presenting the figure of man.

Apollonius speaks of measuring "the city, its gateways, and its wall," but gives no measurements of the gateways, for the obvious reason that is unnecessary since the word "gateway" (pylon, from pyle, "an orifice") sufficiently indicates their nature: They are the twelve orifices of the body.

In the Upanishads, the human body is often called poetically the twelve-gate city.

The "wall" of the city is the aura of the body.

CHAPTER NO. 14

The Drama

In literary construction, the Apocalypse follows to some extent the model of the Greek drama; but in narrative form, it divides into acts, or scenes, in each of which the scenic setting is vividly pictured; and interspersed with the action are monologues, dialogues, and choruses.

As a mere literary device, these scenes are symbolized in a series of visions; and in this Apollonius adopted the style of the Hebrew seers, from whom he obtained much of the quaint symbolism, ornate imagery, and mystifying phraseology he used.

With the material obtained from this source, Apollonius skillfully combined the symbols drawn from the Greeks, the Egyptians, Chaldiac, and other systems, weaving these materials into a harmonious whole.

By sentimental literalists, the Apocalypse is accepted as a record of visions actually seen by "the Seer of Patmos." The visionary style was merely an artifice adopted by Apollonius for the purpose of introducing the fabulous characters of his drama and puzzling his readers.

The Apocalypse is, as its title implies, an account of the initiation of Apollonius himself. In the subtitle, he terms it "the Initiation of Anointed Iesos," that is, of his own illumined Nous, the "witness" for the universal Logos, Solar Man, as Apollonius in the material world, the "slave" of the true Self, is the "witness" for the individual Logos.

Many actors, apparently, appear and play their parts in the drama; yet in reality there is but one performer--the neophyte himself, the sacrificial "Lamb," who awakens all the slumbering forces of his deeper nature, passes thru the terrible ordeals of the purifactory discipline and the telestic labors, and finally emerges as the Conqueror, the self-perfected Man who has regained his standing among the deathless Gods.

He is the hero of, and the sole actor in, the drama; all the other dramatis personae are only personifications of the principles, forces, and elements of Man, the Microcosm so vast and mysterious, whose ultimate destiny is coextensive with the illimitable universe.

First Born from the Dead

In the brief prologue to the drama, the Anointed Iesos, the illuminated Mind, is depicted as the first-born from the dead (the moribund inner faculties) the ruler of the lower powers, yet having been crucified by them on the Cross of Matter (the physical body).

Now, at his coming, they who wounded him shall weep and wail over him.

In the New Testament allegory, there are two crucifixions: one relating to Solar Man's descent into matter, the generation of the physical form, and the other to its ascent to Solarity, or regeneration in the Solar Body.

Then, "in the Breath," that is in the sacred trance, Ioannes has a vision of the Logos (his own solar self), in the self-luminous pneumatic body, of which he gives a magnificent description, partly literal and partly symbolical.

He sees himself walking to and fro among seven little lampstands and holding in his right hand seven stars, announcing himself to be the ever-living Self, who became "dead" (incarnated), but is now alive (as the Solar Man) throughout the aeons, the Logos explaining that the lampstands are the "seven Societies in Asia," and the seven stars their Divinities.

That is, they represent respectively the seven Rays of the Light of the Logos (seven forces) and the seven chakras in the body, thru which they energize.

Asia was the native land of Apollonius, therefore typifying the body, the homeland of Solar Man; and the seven Societies (chakras) are designated by the names of Asian cities, each of which, by some well-known characteristic, or something for which it was noted, called to mind the center of the body which it represents.

To each of these Societies the Logos sends a message; and in them the nature and function of each chakra is indicated; a particular aspect of the Logos is presented to each, a good and a bad quality being ascribed to each chakra, and a prize is promised, specifying the solarical results accuring to "the Conqueror" from the conquest of each chakra.

In the next vision is shown Solar Man enthroned in the sky with his four septenary powers.

Here Apollonius has constructed a simple puzzle by using redundant symbols and by inverting the order of the forces, enumerating the lesser ones first and the greater last.

He places twenty-four Ancients ("elders") circling the throne, before which also are seven Breaths ("spirits") and a crystalline sea; after which he describes four Zoa (little animals), each of which has six wings. He later makes it apparent that the Zoa are superior to the Ancients and next in rank to the Logos. In fact, the four Zoa are the four manifested Powers of the Logos, the archetypes of the four "Beasts," whose nature, as the regents of the four divisions of the body, has already been explained.

As the Zoa are septenates, they have six wings each. These wings are identical with the twenty-four Ancients; and the seven Breaths before the throne are likewise identical with the highest septenate, the noetic Zoon.

This seemingly complicated assemblage thus resolves itself simply into the Nous (Solar Man) centered in the brain with its four septenary powers; and the "glassy sea" is the ether pulsating in the mystic "eye" of the seer. For the "sky" in the Apocalypse is not the "heaven" of the church, the celestial world alleged to be somewhere in the far depths of space.

The four Zoa are the Lion, the Bull, the Man, and the Eagle, which constitute the Sphinx, and represent the four cardinal signs of the zodiac, constituting the "cross" of the zodiac; Leo, Taurus, Aquarius (water-man) and Scorpio. The constellation Aquila, the Eagle, though extra-zodiacal, rising at the same time as Scorpio, is frequently substituted for it.

A scroll (book) is the next symbol introduced. It represents the body, esoterically considered: it is "written inside and at the back," referring to the sympathetic and the cerebro-spinal nerve systems and "sealed with seven seals," which are the seven major chakras, the seven cells of the Vital Battery.

The sacrificial Lamb is the neophyte who has attained to the intuitive, noetic consciousness, which is symbolized by his having seven horns and seven eyes, that is, the seven sense powers of action and perception. He opens the seals (activates the chakras) successively.

As the seals are opened, they change to zodiacal signs, the zodiac being applied to the microcosm (man).

The seven planets are assigned to the twelve signs of the zodiac in the order followed by all ancient and modern authorities.

In Sanscrit writings, the planets are made to correspond also to the seven chakras in the following order, beginning with the Muladhara: Saturn, Jupiter, Mars, Venus, Mercury, Moon, and Sun.

According to this zodiacal arrangement, seven signs, with their planets, extend along the cerebro-spinal region and correspond to the seven chakras, which are the focal centers of the tattvas and have the same planets; while the remaining signs pertain to the five pranas.

Tattvas--the subtle essence of the five elements: earth, water, fire, air, and ether.

Five Pranas--Prana, Apana, Vyana, Samana, Udana (five phases of solar radiation).

The opening of the seven seals by the Lamb will be noticed later.

The sole performers in the Apocalyptic Drama are Solar Man, Psychic Man, Mental Man, Physical Man, Cosmic Elements, Cosmic Creations, and Cosmic Processes. Some of these assume various roles.

The ancient zodiac was subdivided into sections of ten degrees each, called decans, giving three to each of the twelve signs; and to each of these thirty-six subdivisions was assigned an extra-zodiacal constellation, a paranatellion, which rises or sets simultaneously with it.

These forty-eight constellations, twelve in the zodiac and three sets of twelve beyond it, with the Sun considered as the center and making up the number forty-nine, completed the stellar scheme of the zodiac, which is faithfully followed by Apollonius in the Apocalypse.

The seven sacred planets play their parts in the drama; but they only represent seven aspects of the Sun.

The extra-zodiacal constellations Draco, Cetus, Medusa, and Crater are especially prominent as characters in the drama.

Solar Man, the First Logos, takes no active part and is but a voice speaking from the throne.

It should be born in mind that these are the worlds and forces of the Microcosm, man, as portrayed in the zodiacal scheme; and, as the two triangles representing the conflicting solarical and physical principles in the body, they should be considered as being interlaced in man, the "Perfect Square," and enclosed within the auric pleroma.

The Four Planes

In the Apocalypse, the four planes of existence are represented as (1) the Sky, (2) the Rivers and Springs, (3) the Sea, and (4) the Earth. Encompassing these four is the Air, the Empyrean, called the Fifth World in the Ptolemaic system, although it really represents the three formless planes.

The twelve forces active on each of the four manifested planes, or worlds of form, are divided into a five and a seven. The five is subdivided into a one and a four; and the seven is subdivided into a three and a four, the three being subdivided into a one and a two.

These divisions, written diagrammatically as if on a measuring-stick, make the "rod" with which to "measure the adytum of the God (Solar Man), the altar, and those who worship in it," excluding the court which is exterior to the adytum.

The "measuring stick" applies to each of the four manifested planes; and in each of them the fivefold group relates to the Sun and the Rectors of the Four Regions of Space, symbolizing variously Solar Man and his four manifested powers, the Nous and the four intellective faculties, etc. The sevenfold group relates to the Moon (feminine principle) and her septenary time-periods.

The fivefold group, which is really a quaternary and a dominating power, corresponds in each case to the Arche-Logos (True Being).

The Drama Has Seven Acts

The Apocalyptic Drama has seven acts, as follows:

1. The Opening of the seven seals, the conquest of the seven cells of the Human Battery.

2. The sounding of the seven trumpets, the conquest of the seven centers of the cerebro-spinal system that correspond to the seven cells of the battery.

3. The sky battle, representing the expulsion of the Dragon and his Divinities, i.e., the elimination from the Mind of all impure thoughts.

4. The harvesting of the earth and its vine, the quest of the seven cardiac centers.

5. The out-pouring of the seven scourges, the conquest of the procreative centers, which concludes the "conquest of the chakras," and, according to the ancient doctrine, produces the birth of the Solar Body.

6. The battle in the psychic world, or infernal region, called Armageddon, resulting in the subjugation of the three beasts; i.e., the extinction of the extraneous phantasmal demon, or composite elemental self.

7. The last judgment, which means a summing up of the completed cycle of earth lives.

All the remaining portions of the Apocalypse are explanatory and descriptive.

All these seven acts, four (conquest of the chakras) relate to the four divisions of the body, and the other three to the mental, psychic, and auric principles.

In a general way, the Four Conquests correspond to the Four Seasons. The opening of the seals, the beginning of man's solarical resurrection, is Spring, the time of germinating seed, expanding bud, and upspringing vegetation.

The energizing of the noetic centers, the trumpet-calls awakening to life the sunlike intellectual faculties, is Summer, the season of sturdy growth and developing to ripeness, the ever-fervid sun, at times, scorching the tender-green growth. (Note: Too much sunshine is bad for man.)

The opening of the heart-centers, the harvesting of the earth and vine, is Autumn, the period of gathering and garnering the fruitage.

The conquest of the lower life-centers, the scourging of all that is base and impure in man's nature, is Winter, the season of purifying frost and freeze, which prevails until the returning Sun, the lengthening of the days, is mystically Reborn as the Sun God of a new year, the aeon of the deified man, the Savior of the World, distorted by the church and personified in its Jesus.

The perfection of the Apocalyptic Drama is amazing. It is expressed in terms of cosmic phenomena. Its hero is the Sun (male principle), its heroine the Moon (female principle), and all its other characters are Planets, Stars, and Constellations; while its stage-setting comprises the Sky, the Earth, the Rivers, and the Sea.

The Apocalypse elucidates its subject with the roll of thunder, emphasizes it with the shock of the earthquake and reiterates it with the ceaseless murmur of its "many waters." It always maintains this Cosmic Language, this vast phrasing of nature, and it must have taken the Ancient Masters years to perfectionize it.

In the first magnificent chorus of Constellations that encircle the throne of the Sun God, the heavenly hosts praise Him as the Creator of the Universe. Yet when the drama is concluded, that Universe has perished, "the first sky and the first earth are passed away, and the sea exists no more." (Rev. 21:1).

Taken from his effulgent throne, the Sun God announces, "Behold! I am making a new Universe." (Rev. 21:5).

This new Universe is Redeemed Man, the lesser cosmos, the Microcosm, of whom the Sun, Moon, Planets, and all the Stars of the Universe are in truth the Architect and Builder, the moulder and the maker.

For in every man, however fallen and degraded, are contained all the forces which brought him into being and have nurtured him throughout the vast cycle of generation.

Zodiac and Apocalypse

The Ancient Masters discovered what Darwin asserted, that all things in the Universe are related and that the Solarical History of Man has been exacted on a cosmic scale in the Starry Sky ages before it was repeated on Earth in the Human Drama.

So the Zodiac was the Grand Symbol of the sacred Science of the Lemurian Masters hundreds of thousands of years ago.

After the Zodiac Plan was prepared, the Apocalypse was written in symbol and parable in order to record for future ages an explanation of the Zodiac Symbolism so that its secret wisdom would not be lost.

CHAPTER NO. 15

THE APOCALYPSE
(The Hindu Scroll)

The title, "The Initiation of Ioannes," was invented by Apollonius without doubt. The sub-title presents "The Anointed Iesous" as the candidate for initiation.

Ioannes and Iesous are but one person, the former indicating physical man and the latter Solar Man, the real noetic Self. The former must truly become the "slave" of the latter if he would reach the goal of the Seer.

The Divinity who appears at the behest of Iesous represents the Creative Power and remains in the drama as the Hierophant or Initiator, while Ieosus, the candidate, is subjected to the initiatory ordeals and performs the "perfecting works," whereby he finally becomes the Conqueror on the white horse--the new Initiate in his Solar Body.

The perfections have to be attained "speedily" by sustained, unremitting effort. Yet, as time is considered by those who regard earth-life as an event of but one incarnation, the telestic work would seem by no means expeditious. For it requires not less than seven incarnations of untiring effort before the final goal is reached, according to the Ancient Masters.

But the Royal Road of the esotericists is a short-cut and his, a speedy journey, as compared with the progress of those who are content to follow the common highway of evolution and who will reach their final destination, their "promised land," only after ages of aimless wandering in the wilderness of terrestrial life.

It is the intuitive mind, "Anointed Iesous," that presents evidence of the Creative Power to the neophyte, and he in turn, according to the law of the occult must transmit it to his fellowmen who usually reward him with some form of physical or mental martyrdom.

With this prelude we shall proceed to interpret "The Revelation of St. John The Divine," but not according to the word and letter of the authorized version.

Our interpretation is based broadly upon the undisputed meaning of the Greek text, which the clever priest worked over in order to make it acceptable to the church.

He who is that much interested may discover how greatly the Greek Text was distorted by comparing the version appearing here with the authorized version in the Bible.

Chapter 1: 1, 2

The initiation of Anointed Iesous, which the Hierophant conferred on him to make known to his slaves the (perfections) which must be attained speedily. He sent his Divinity and by him symbolized (them) to his slave Ioannes, who gave evidence of the Logos of the Hierophant and of the evidence of Anointed Iesous, of all the (secrets) that he saw.

Interpretation

In the Greek Mysteries, which were also termed the "perfecting" or "Finishing" rites, the candidates for initiation, after receiving some preparatory training in semi-exoteric lesser rites, were termed mystai (veiled ones), while the Initiates were called epoptai (those having super-sight, seers).

The Greek word apokalypsis (unveiling) is clearly a substitute for epopteia, "initiation into seership."

Ch. 1:3

Immortal is he who discerns and they who learn (from him), the arcane doctrine of this Teaching and observe the (precepts) which are written in it; for (their) season is near.

Interpretation

This is a dedication of the book to every mystic who may succeed in penetrating to its inner meaning and impart to other students the occult doctrines it contains.

Ch. 1: 4, 5

Ioannes to the seven Societies which are in Asia; Grace to you and peace, from (Solar Man) who (forever) is, who was, and who is coming, and from the seven Breaths that are before his throne and from Anointed Iesous, that believable witness, the first-born from "the dead," and the foremost of the rulers of the earth.

Interpretation

The seven Societies symbolize the Seven Seals, Cells, Chakras, of the body. Later they are metamorphosed into "seven little lampstands," each chakra being a little brain, a minor light-giver in the body, as the brain is the great light-giver, or microcosmic sun; and then they are changed almost directly into "seven seals" on a scroll, the chakras being indeed sealed in the average person so far as their psychic functions are concerned.

The word "coming" is used because the future participle of the verb "to be" would convey an erroneous metaphysical concept; "was," in the imperfect tense, expresses an action still continuing, but the future "shall be," would imply something that does not yet exist, whereas Solar Man is represented as subsisting in an infinite Present which includes in itself the Past and the Future.

A similar statement appears in the John, which expresses the same idea in these words, "Before Abraham was born, I am" (8:58). In other words, before earth-man Abraham was born, Solar Man "was."

The seven Breaths which appear later as seven stars (seven planets) are the seven psychic powers.

Iesous, the first-born from "the dead" represents the epistemonic (intuitive) Mind; the intuition is the first of man's dormant solar faculties to awaken, bringing certainty of knowledge and becoming the dominant power in his life.

Ch. 1: 5, 6

To him who, having graciously welcome us and washed us from our sins in his blood, also made us rulers and sacrificers to his God, to him be the glory and dominion throughout the aeons of the aeons!--Amen.

Interpretation

These words refer to the initiation Ioannes (physical man) has gone thru and which he is about to describe. The lustration (baptismos) of blood which emancipates from sin is the rain of purifying fire poured out by the Divinities charged with the seven scourges, which we shall reach in due time.

By a simile, a variant of the parable of the prodigal son (lu. 15:11-32), the higher Self is represented as hospitably entertaining the returned wanderer, the reincarnating self, and washing from him the stains of travel.

To each of the planets a distinctive attribute is assigned; and here "dominion" applies to the Sun and "glory" to the Moon.

The Amen is the Greek equivalent of the Sanscrit Aum, the latter being pronounced with a nasal prolongation, called ardha-matri, "half measure," thus giving the Apocalyptic "time, (two) times and a half a time."

Used in a certain way, this word was said to have the power, through the correlation of sound and the vital electricity, to awaken the Serpentine Fire. To use it effectively, one must know not only its correct pronunciation, but also the predominant color and the key-note of his own aura. This perhaps is more Hindu magic used to mislead the unwary.

Ch. 1:7

Behond! He comes admist the clouds, and every eye shall see him and they who pierced him (shall see him); and all the tribes of the earth shall wail over him. Verily! Amen.

INTERPRETATION

The eyes that see him are the seven chakras; they who "pierced him" are the sense-perceptions; and the "tribes" are the repentant elements of the mental and psychic constitution.

The "clouds" are the auric forces. Here the nimbus seems to be referred to rather than the aureola; the latter envelopes the entire body, while the nimbus is limited to the head.

Ch. 1: 8

"I am the Alpha and the O," says the Master, the Solar God, who (forever) is, who was, and who is coming, the All-Dominator.

INTERPRETATION

This formula includes the five intermediate vowels, E, H, I, O, and T, and is equivalent to saying, "I am the seven vowels in one," and refers to the Seven Planetary Powers which are potential in the First Logos. In the Second Logos, they become manifested potencies.

The title "All-Dominator" is solar. The sun dominates all the planets.

Ch. 1: 9-11

I, Ioannes, who am your brother, as also your copartner in the ordeal, ruling and patience of Iesous, came to be in the island which is called Patmos, thru the arcane doctrine of the Solar God and thru the evidence of Iesous. I came to be in the Breath (-trance) on the mastery-day, and I heard behind me a loud voice, like a trumpet-call, saying:

"What you see, write in a scroll; and send (the message) to the seven Societies which are in Asia: to Ephesos, Smyrna, Pergamos, Thyateira, Sardeis, Philadelpheia, and Laodikeia."

INTERPRETATION

Serene patience is one of the indispensable qualifications of the aspirant for solarical knowledge and so is the "ruling," or dominance of the higher intellect, the Nous (Iesous), over the lower faculties. The ordeal is that of initiation, now begun.

Thru the awakening noetic perception (the "evidence of Iesous") and the increasing light from the Logos—the whitening of the dawn of the new life—the aspirant becomes isolated, and in the loneliness of one who has forever abandoned the illusions of sensuous existence, but has not yet seen the sunrise of the Solar Man, he dwells, as it were, on an island, apart from his fellow-men.

Then thru his introspection comes the message of the Great Breath; and in the sacred trance, he attains his first autopsia, beholding the apparition of his own Logos, very similar to a man who sees himself in a dream.

Ch. 1: 12-16

I turned about to see the Voice which was speaking with me. Having turned, I saw seven little golden lampstands; and in the midst of the lampstands, an (apparition) like the son of man, wearing (a vesture) reaching to the feet and girded at the paps with a golden girdle. His head and his hair were white as white wool, (white) as snow; and his eyes were as a blaze of fire. His feet were like the liquid-metal that is as if it had been melted in a furnace. His voice was as the voice of many waters. In his right hand, he had seven stars. From his mouth kept flashing forth a keen two-edged sword. His face was (luminous), as shines the sun by its inherent force.

INTERPRETATION

This apparition is a fanciful picture of the Sun, or fount of all-radiating light; and, like all the puzzles of Apollonius, it is ingeniously constructed.

The "voice" that speaks is the primary aspect of the Second Logos, in whom the seven "voices" or vowels (for phone is the one Greek word for both "vowel" and "voice") become differentiated.

As the all-pervading solar Light, he walks about among the seven golden lampstands, the seven planetary bodies, holding in his right hand their seven "stars," the light which he confers upon them.

The Logos-figure described is a composite picture of the seven sacred planets: he has the white hair of Kronos ("Father Time"), the blazing eyes of "wide-seeing" Zeus, the sword of Ares, the shining face of Helios, and the chiton and girdle of Aphrodite; his feet are of mercury, the metal sacred to Hermes, and his voice is like the murmur of the ocean is waves, alluding to Selene, the Moon-Goddess of the four seasons and of the waters.

The material, mercury, used in fabricating the feet of the Planetary Logos, were ranked by the ancient as a primary metal next to gold, as "a sort of bright and condensed fluid." The word is rendered "fine brass" in the authorized version, but brass was unknown to the ancient Greeks who used a bronze composed of copper and tin.

The figure of the Sun as a ruler of the planets is a symbol of the incarnated Solar Man; and, as recorded in the description of the apparition, the seven planets are in reverse order, for the Second Logos (terrestrial man) is the inverted reflection of the First (celestial man), who is, as it were, upside-down when incarnated in the physical world. The significance of this inversion appears later in the drama.

"Son of man" are words to be found in Ezekiel, Zechariah, and Daniel, but while similar, they are not the same; for the Apocalypse is sui generis (of its own kind); and while Apollonius borrowed many symbols and poetic images from ancient writings, he usually employs them to conceal his real meaning by endowing them with a different of a variant significance.

This interpretation of the Hindu Scroll is not concerned with the esotericism of the Hebrew scriptures in the Bible, and the usual references to them woven into the Apocalypse will be omitted.

Ch. 1: 17-20

When I saw him, I fell at his feet as one dead. He placed his right hand on me, saying:

"Be not afraid. I am the First (Adam) and the Last (Adam), he (Solar Man) who is Alive. I became a "dead man" (incarnated); and, Behold! I am alive throughout the aeons of the aeons, and I have the keys of Death and of the Unseen.

"Write down the (glories) you saw, also those which are and those which are about to be attained next after them (beginning with) the mystery of the seven stars which you saw on my right hand and the seven little golden lampstands. The seven stars are the Divinities of the seven Societies; and the seven little lampstands are the seven Societies.

INTERPRETATION

The esoteric tenet as to "the First and the Last" is stated by Apollonius in 1 Cor. 15:22-45:

"For even as in the Adam (-man) all become moribund, so likewise in the Solar (-man) all are restored to life." Which simply means that as Solar Man is imprisoned and bound in the flesh, when the form of flesh perishes, Solar Man is freed from the earthy prison and lives again as before incarnation.

This is the mystery mentioned by Apollonius in these words: "Behold, I show you a mystery: We shall not sleep (in death), but we shall all be changed (to solar life in a moment, in the twinkling of an eye" (1 Cor. 15:51, 52).

Passing thru this "born again" process, Apollonius mentions as "our light affliction, which is but for a moment, (and) worketh for us a far more exceeding and eternal weight of glory" (2 Cor. 4:17).

The Masters considered Solar Man "dead" during incarnation; and when "born again" thru the creative process termed "death," Solar Man knows that he has the keys of Death and of the Unseen.

The Representation of incarnated life as the death-like obscuration of Solar Man is very common in ancient mystical literature.

In Part I of this work, we noticed the symbolical meaning of seven Societies or the seven Cities (churches) in Asia Minor.

The seven small lampstands are the Seven Chakras, and their "stars" are the differentiated forces of the Solar Fire.

CHAPTER NO. 16

Ch. 2: 1-7

"To the Divinity of the Society in Ephesus write:

"These (words) says he who with his right hand dominates the seven stars, he who walks about in the midst of the seven little golden lampstands: I know your works and your over-toil and patience, and that you cannot bear wicked men. You put to the test those pretending to be apostles and found them false. You endured and have patience; on account of my name, you have toiled and have not grown weary. But I have (this complaint) against you, that you left your first love. Remember, therefore, whence you are fallen; reform, and do the first works--but if not, coming to you speedily, I shall move your lampstand out of its place, unless you do reform. But you have this (virtue), that you abhor the works of the Nikolaitanes, which I also abhor. He who has an ear, let him hear what the Breath is saying to the Societies.

"The Conqueror--to him I shall award to eat (the fruit) of the tree of life which is in the middle of the Garden of the God."

INTERPRETATION

To this Society the Solar Man announces himself in his aspect as Memory, the faculty of receiving and retaining impressions, which links together the past, present, and future, and is thus the power upon which depends the continuity of the individual consciousness.

The ever-toiling and unwearied memory stores up all the experiences of the individual, throughout the long cycle of incarnations; and no memories are ever lost save those that are evil and therefore suffer the "second death" after the final purification of Solar Man.

The muladhara chakra, represented by Ephesus, lies at the base of the spine, and being thus at the lower pole of the cerebro-spine system and the starting-point of the sushumna chakra, it is directly related to the highest, the sahasrara chakra, or the conarium; for, as we have said, the lower level of life is the inverted reflection of the higher. Hence it is said to have left its first love (the divine love having become human love), and is told to remember whence it has fallen and do the first works, i.e., pour its kundalini force into the first and highest chakra, the brain-center.

The quality of this chakra still retains somewhat of the higher love, a clinging to purity and an aversion to sensuality and every perversion of the creative function. It is therefore said to have exposed the impure charlatans and to abhor the works (secret rites) of the Nikolaitanes.

The latter were a pseudo-occult sect that practiced the vilest forms of phallic sorcery. The unclean worship of the "Great Mother," called Rhea, Cybele, Astarte, Isis, and by other names, was widespread in Asia; and many were her temples, with their "consecrated women." But in the older mythology, Rhea was not thus degraded.

The attainment of "spiritual" knowledge is in effect the process of reviving the memory of the incarnating Solar Man in relation to the supernal worlds before he became immured, imprisoned in matter. This memory of things antecedent can be recalled only through the action of the Serpentine Fire, the generative force. Hence in this aspect, Solar Man is said to hold in his grasp the seven stars and to walk among the seven little lampstands.

As the sun enters each sign of the zodiac, it is said, astrologically, to conquer the sign and to assimilate its particular quality. The same is said of the Kundalini as it flows thru the chakras. Hence, the hero of the drama, who is the Microcosmic Sun, is called The Conqueror.

The award to the Conqueror, in the aspect here presented, is the Eternal Memory: He shall eat the fruit of the tree of life (the fruitage of the life-cycle) in the God's own abiding-place, the mystical Paradise, or state of ineffable bliss.

In this aspect the Logos is Kronos, the God of Time.

Ch. 2: 8-11

"To the Divinity of the Society in Smyrna write:

"These (words) say the First (Adam) and the Last (Adam), who became a 'dead man,' and came to life: I know your ordeal and poverty (but you are rich!) and the profanity of those claiming to be Ioudaians--and they are not, but are an assembly of the Adversary. Do not fear the (ordeals) which are you about to undergo. Behold! The Accuser is about to cast some of you into prison, that you may be brought to trial; and you will have an ordeal of ten days. Become confiding until death, and I shall give you the crown of life. He who has an ear, let him hear what the Breath is saying to the Societies.

"The Conqueror shall not at all be punished by the second death!"

INTERPRETATION

Here the Logos is presented in his aspect as Reason, the highest philosophical intellection (noesis), which is the carnal man is dormant, but which awakens when he turns to the serious consideration of the concerns of the higher life.

The reasoning faculty, hampered by the material brain, is poverty-stricken; but when freed from the trammels of matter, it is rich in ideas.

The pseudo-Ioudaians are the irrational dogmas of exoteric religion, put forth as divine revelations, yet they are obviously opposed to reason and are but the mere vagaries of the perverted devotional nature and therefore come not from the Logos but from his adversary, Satanas, the foe of intellectual light.

The "ten days" refer to a zodiacal decan and a paranatellon--here, the constellation Draco (the Great Red Dragon), who is the prosecutor or accuser, the passion in the blood.

This chakra, the Svadhishthana, is the starting-point of Ida and Pingala Nadis, allegorized as the "two witnesses," the sushumna being the third. The ordeals "which you are about to undergo" means the rising of the solar fire.

The Conqueror shall not be punished by the second death means Conscious Immortality: He is to wear the crown of life, and nothing that originates in the psychic mind shall pass into the obligion of the second death.

Ch. 2: 12-17

"To the Divinity of the Society in Pergamos write:

"These (words) says he who has the keen two-edged sword: I know your works and where you dwell—where the throne of the Adversary is. You are holding fast my name, and you did not abjure belief in me even in the days in which (the oracle was) Antipas, my believable witness, who was slain among you, where the Adversary dwells. But I have a few (complaints) against you, because you have there those who uphold the teaching of Balaam, who taught Balak to set a snare before the children of Israel, to eat (food) offered to ghosts, and to prostitute. So, also, you have those who uphold the teachings of the Nikolaitanes, which I abhor. Reform—but if not, coming to you speedily, I shall combat them with the sword of my mouth. He who has an ear, let him hear what the Breath is saying to the Societies.

"The Conqueror—to him I shall award to eat a share of the occult menna; and I shall award to him a white voting-pebble, and on the voting-pebble (will be) a new name engraved, which no one knows but he who receives it."

INTERPRETATION

In this case, the Logos presents himself in his aspect as Will, volition, energizing principle, and therefore carries the sword of the War-God.

Pergamos represents the Manipura Chakra, solar plexus, chief center of the sympathetic nervous system, the seat of the epithumetic nature, the Dragon, the Adversary of the Logos. This is also the "witness Antipas."

The snare of Palak, the eating of food devoted to "spirits," and sexual promiscuity, all refer to various goetic practices, the nature of which is best left unexplained.

The double-edged sword indicates the Good and Evil aspects of the generative force controlled by the abdominal brain, the Manipura Chakra region. The results depend upon the use made of this double-edged force.

The reward to the Conqueror, who by his will-power vanquishes all the evil foes of his own nature and fights his way against the passions of his blood to the region of Light, is that he has imparted to him the secret wisdom of the Masters and is awarded a white voting-pebble with a new name engraved thereon, which indicates he has been named and naturalized a member of the Order of the Initiated.

Here the Logos has the semblance of Ares (Mars), corresponding to the vowel O, and the attribute "force."

Ch. 2: 18-29

"To the Divinity of the Society in Thyateira, write:

"These (words) say the son of the God, who has his eyes as a blaze of fire and his feet like the liquid metal: I know your works and your love, belief, service, and patience; and that your last works (are to be) greater than your first ones. But I have (a complaint) against you, that you tolerate the woman Iezabel, who, professing to be a seeress, teaches and deludes my slaves to prostitute and to eat (food) offered to ghosts. I have her time, that she might reform; but she does not will to reform from prostitution. Behold! I throw her down on a (stick-) bed, and those committing adultery with her (I shall subject) to a grievous ordeal, unless they shall reform from their works. I shall slay her children in the Death (-world); and all the Societies shall know that I am he who searches into kidneys and hearts. I shall give (awards) to each of you according to your works. But to you I say, to the rest in Thyateira--as many do not possess this teaching, who remained guiltless of knowledge concerning the depths of the Adversary, as they say--I do not cast on you an additional burden. Nevertheless, that which you do possess, retain dominion over it till I come.

"The Conqueror--who also observes my works until the perfecting period--to him I shall award authority over the people, and he will rule them with an iron wand (like vessels of clay they are being crushed!) as I also received (authority) from my father. And I shall award to him the morning star. He who has an ear, let him hear what the Breath is saying to the Societies.

INTERPRETATION

This area is the Anahata chakra; and to this center the Logos presents himself in his aspect as Direct Cognition, the faculty of apprehending truth without the aid of inductive reasoning; and in this aspect as the Sun, the pure intellectual effulgence, he is not the "son of man," but the "son of the Sun," having the all-seeing eyes of Zeus and the winged feet of Hermes, thus combining the attributes of the higher psychic consciousness.

(Note: It is not the liver but the solar plexus nerve ganglion that is the reflector of the mind in the epithumetic region; nor is it the heart but the cardiac plexus nerve ganglion that is the reflector of the mind and the center of the higher psychic consciousness. But our interpretation is based on the theories of the Masters. Hotema.)

The corresponding reflector in the brain is the conarium; and the generative organs, the "three witnesses," or inverted analogue of the higher triad, fulfill the same psychic function in the lowest of the four somatic divisions; hence the allusion to the "kidneys" or "loins"--an euphemism for gonad glands. (Note: the prostate gland (kanda) should be included--Hotema.)

The four virtues enumerated, love, belief, service, and patience, correspond to the four noetic qualities transmitted through the heart (not the heart but the thymus gland--Hotema).

The pseudo-seeress Iezabel has the name and attributes of the sorceress, Ahab's wife, of malodorous memory, in the Old Testament fable.

Here she represents the emotional erotic sort of psychism which is sometimes developed at orgiastric "religious revivals," and which is more characteristic of hysterical women than of rational persons.

By this prostitution of mind and emotion to the base epithumetic nature, causing moral disintegration and dissipation of psychic energy, mediumistic faculties are sometimes developed, opening up avenues of communication with the "shades of the dead," the disgusting larvae to whom the misguided medium quite literally offers as food the elements of his own disintegrating personality.

The award to the Conqueror--if he also heeds the works of the Logos, that is, observes the admonitions of the psychic mind--is the absolute dominion over the lower faculties and forces of his body, which he rules as with a rod of iron; and he receives the morning star, which symbolizes the Divine Love that heralds the coming day full of solaristical illumination.

Here the Logos has the aspect of Helios (Sun); the corresponding vowel is I, and the attributes, three in number, are dominion, wealth, and thanks, or all-graciousness, the latter epithet implying that the Solar Logos unites in himself all the graces or good qualities of the seven sacred planets.

CHAPTER NO. 17

Ch. 3: 1-6

"To the Divinity of the Society in Sardeis write:

"These (words) says he who has the seven Breaths of the God and the seven stars: I know your works; that you have the name that you are alive, but that you are a dead man. Become awakened (from the dead) and strengthen the remaining (affections) that are on the point of dying; for I have not found your works accomplished before my God. Therefore, remember how you have received (this message) and heard (it); and observe (its precepts), and reform. If, therefore, you will not be awake, I shall come upon you (silently) as a thief (comes), and you will not know what hour I shall come upon you. But you have a few names in Sardeis who did not sully their garments, and they shall walk with me in white (rainment), for they are deserving.

"The Conqueror--he shall thus be clothed in white garments, and I shall not erase his name from the book of Life, but I shall acknowledge his name before my Father and before his Divinities."

INTERPRETATION

The Logos here proclaims himself in his aspect as Divine Love, the deific creative force; and here he is the synthesis of the seven planets (stars) and the seven creative forces (pneumata), thus corresponding somewhat to the First Logos, or Eros.

Sardeis represents the Vishuddi chakra, the throat region, which is directly related to the lower creative centers, as is shown by the change of voice at the time of puberty, and the castrato voice of the eunuch.

The throat, the thyroid area, is also peculiarly affected by the finer emotions.

This higher love is here said to have the name of being alive, yet to be dead in reality. For the devotional aspirations and purer affections of humanity are pitifully weak.

It is this deadness of the moral feelings that stills the voice of conscience; yet at any time that conscience may unexpectedly speak out, bringing remorse and sorrow to him whom the Self has thus suddenly aroused, coming upon him silently, as a thief in the night. This simile is repeated in Chapter 16, vs. 15, with almost identical wording.

Sardeis was a center of Venus-worship, having a temple to Astarte.

The reward to the Conqueror is perfect purity (Son of Perfection), and the auric color corresponding to this chakra (its esoteric "name") will remain in the aureola (book of life), or "glory", emotions becoming transmuted into the eternal happiness.

In this aspect, the Logos is Aphrodite (Venus), the Goddess of Love. It is only in this female aspect that the Logos is the creative "Word" (in one sense the occult potency of sound), and therefore identical with Vach, "speech," who is also Sarasvati (Venus) in Hindu mythology. The corresponding vowel is H, and the attributes are invocation and realm, or ruling.

Ch. 3: 7-13

"To the Divinity of the Society in Philadelpheia write:

"These (words) says he who is Holy, who is True, who has David's key, who opens and no one shall shut, who shuts and no one opens: Behold! I have swung open before you a door that no one can shut. For (I know) that you have a little force; and you observed my arcane doctrine and did not abjure my name. I am giving (Deliverance to some of you) from among the assembly of the Adversary (composed) of those professing to be Ioudaians--and they are not, but are lying. I shall cause them to come and make obeisance before your feet and to know that I have graciously received you. Because you from the (first) hour of that probation which is about to come upon the entire homeland, to put to the proof those who are dwelling upon the earth. I am coming speedily. Retain a firm grasp on the (steadfast virtue) which you possess, so that no one may carry off your crown.

"The Conqueror--I shall make him a pillar in the adytum of my God, and never more shall he go outside of it; and I shall write on him the name of my God and the name of the city of my God, the new Jerusalem, which is coming down out of the sky from my God; and (I shall write on him) my new name."

INTERPRETATION

Here the Logos presents the aspect of Divine Thought, the pure and unmixed nature of intellect, or the unrefracted light of the Nous--thought not differentiated into thoughts, but considered as the energizing principle of Mind and the complement of the energizing principle of Love.

"The Holy" and "the True" are identical with "the Good" and "the True" of Plato, while the correlated Aphrodite-aspect is "the Beautiful."

According to Kaballistic mysticism, ADAM represents Adam, David, and Messias, making the Messias the reincarnation of Adam and of David: these represent three stages in man's life-cycle, Adam being the primeval state of child-like innocence, David the adolescence in which good and evil struggle for mastery, and Iesous (Messias) the stage of maturity.

David, for all his vileness and evil deeds, had the virile depth of feeling, philosophic breadth of mind, and poetic insight that give promise to Divine Man; and these were his "key" to the door giving entrance to the higher consciousness. (Compare with this ch. 22:16 and interpretation).

Philadelpheia represents the Ajna chakra, center at the forehead. This is the point of divergence of the auric light, the color of which reveals infallibly the solarical status of each person. Thus, if the light radiating from it is golden-yellow, it is the "name" of the Sun; if dull red or green, it is the "brand of the Beast." This relates to whether the Solar Fire is consumed in masturbation and copulation or is conserved to improve body and brain.

The reward of the Conqueror is that he is to become a sustaining power in the higher world, no more to reincarnate, but to abide in the eternal city, the Solar Body.

The aspect of the Logos here is that of Hermes (Mercury), the Master of Occult wisdom. The corresponding vowel is E, and the attributes are Honor and Deliverance.

Ch. 3: 14-22

"To the Divinity of the Society in Laodikeia write:

"These (words) says the Amen, the witness believable and true, the origin of the God's organic world: I know your works, that you are neither cold nor hot. I would that you were cold or hot. So, because of your luke-warmness, neither hot nor cold, I am on the point of vomiting you from my mouth. Because you say, "I am rich, I have become rich, and I have lack of nothing," and do not know that you are the worn-out, pitiable, beggarly, blind, and naked one, I advise you to buy from me gold tried by fire--so that you be rich--and white garments so that you may clothe yourself and the shame of your nakedness not be apparent, and eyesalve to anoint your eyes, so that you may see.

"As many as I love, I confute and instruct. Therefore be emulous and reform. I am standing at the door and gently tapping. If any one hears my voice and opens the door, him I shall visit; and I shall dine with him, and he with me.

"The Conqueror--I shall award to him to be seated with me on my throne, as I also conquered and was seated with my father on his throne."

INTERPRETATION

The Logos here announces himself as the Cosmic Substance, Arche, from which originate all the elements, both subtile and gross, including those forms of matter which modern physicists classify as "forces."

Laodikeia represents the Sahasrara chakra, the atrophied "unpaired eye" of science. Hence the allusion to the Phrygian "eyesalve." This is the Pineal gland.

Neither cold nor hot--having neither the dispassionate reason nor the devotional fervor, but lukewarm and nauseating to the higher mind, the lower mind yet prides itself on its supposed wealth of intellectual attainments; yet, without the gold of solarical refinement and the white garments of purity, these attainments are meager and unlovely.

The reward of the Conqueror is to share the throne of the God, that is, to become one with his own Solarical Self.

Here the Logos has the semblance of Isis (the Moon), the "white-armed" Goddess who rules the four seasons and the waters. The corresponding vowel is A; and the attributes are glory and authority.

*** *** ***

In the seven benedictions contained in the Apocalypse, twelve attributes are given; of these, three are assigned to the sun, two to each of the members of the higher triad, and one to each of the lower.

When the two triads (the sun always being the center) are paralleled, the result in a fourfold system, in which the Divine Faculty (episteme) stands alone and the other faculties are paired.

CHAPTER NO. 18

Ch. 4: 1-3

After these (things) I saw; and Behold! a door opened in the sky; and it was that first voice I (now) heard, like a trumpet--call speaking to me (the enthroned God) saying:

"Come up hither, and I shall make known to you the (things) which must be attained hereafter."

Immediately I came to be in the Breath (-trance), Behold! a throne was placed in the sky; and on the throne (the God) was seated. The enthroned (God) was in appearance like an opal and a carnelian, and a rainbow encircled the throne in appearance like an aquamarine.

INTERPRETATION

The reader observes that we have traced the ascent of the Kundalini Force from the lowest chakra up thru the others, to the Pineal gland in the brain, the area of the Sahasrara chakra, situated in the crown of the head, "the throne of Siva," the seat of "the Nibodhika Fire."

As we reached each chakra in the ascent, we saw that Apollonius had prepared a little fable to describe the general qualities of each area of the body affected and controlled by its respective chakra, as the chakras are activated by the ascending Serpentine Fire.

The Sushumna nadi extends up to the Pineal in the brain and on to "Brahma-randhra," the "hole of Brahma," or the soft spot in the crown of a baby's head. <u>This is the "door opened in the sky."</u>

The mystery of the All-Seeing Eye, which has been poetically expressed as "a window into space," was symbolized in various ways in the ancient world.

In honor of the sacred eye in the crown of the head, the "door" opened in the sky" (Rev. 4:1), the monks of all ancient nations shave off their hair over this spot which is supposed to look out.

Small children that have but recently completed their embryonic recapitulation of humanity's early struggle for life have an unduly sensitive area about the crown of the head. The skull does not close there immediately. In some cases it never closes, although usually the sutures unite between the second and fifth years.

The extreme sensitiveness over the area of the All-Seeing Eye is accompanied by a certain clairvoyance. The small child is still living largely in the invisible worlds, the fourth dimension. While its body is unresponsive, it is conscious and active, at least to a limited degree, in the unseen worlds with which it is connected by the open gateway of the Pineal gland, the "door opened in the sky." Gradually certain manifestations of the higher consciousness enter into the Pineal and crystallize into the fine grit found in the gland. There is no grit in the gland until this consciousness enters.

This tiny grit in the Pineal is a mystery about which modern science knows practically nothing. Investigations have shown that this grit is absent in idiots and others lacking properly organized consciousness of man. It serves as a connecting link between consciousness and the physical body.

Those with discerning eyes will see in the spinal canal extending upward into the chambers of the brain, thru certain gateways concerning which science is ignorant, the channels and chambers of the ancient Mysteries. They will realize that the Golden Fire is the candidate who is being initiated.

The statement, "Come up hither, and I shall make known to you the (things) which must be attained hereafter," refers to the blending of the powers of seeing and hearing, previously mentioned.

The Pineal gland is phosphorescent; and when stimulated by the Creative Fire, it glows and emits electrical waves of a faint roseate hue.

This is the "enthroned God" whose appearance is so colorful, the colors being the electrical emanations flowing from the Pineal as a result of its being stimulated by the Creative Fire of Life, conserved for body and brain improvement instead of being consumed in the common custom of procreation.

Ch. 4: 4-8

Encircling the throne were 24 thrones; and on the thrones (I saw) 24 elders seated, arrayed in white garments, and on their heads golden crowns. From the throne went out lightnings, thunders, and voices; and (there were) seven lamps of fire burning before the throne, which are the seven Breaths of the God. Before the throne (was a sheen) as a glassy sea, like crystal. In the middle of the throne and in a circle about the throne (were) four beings, full of eyes before and behind. The first Being was like a Lion; the second Being was like a young Bull; the third Being had the face of a Man; and the fourth Being was like a flying Ea Eagle. The four Beings, having each one of them six wings, are full of eyes round about and within; and ceaselessly day and night they keep saying:

"Holy, Holy, Holy (is) the Master-God, the All-Dominator, who was, who (forever) is, and who is coming!"

INTERPRETATION

The four Beings represent the Sphinx, and the Sphinx represents the Four Principle or Elements of Creation, as explained in our work titled, "THE MYSTERIOUS SPHINX." (By Hotema - $3.00 from Health Research.)

The Four Principles of Creation are the four great planes of existence and correspond to the four states of seership, on each of those planes. Each of these four states of seership has a subjective and an objective phase on the plane to which it relates; and this is symbolized by the many exterior and interior eyes.

As macrocosmic powers, the four Beasts are mystically the four quarters of the zodiac, the four arms, so to say, of the sun; and as solar forces, each is a septenate, radiating from a focal point into the six directions of space.

Similarly, the time-periods are divided into fourths, as the year, which has four seasons, each containing three months, these being again subdivided into bright and dark fortnights, making 24 such periods, corresponding to the 24 hours of the day.

The forces which, whether in the macrocosm or the microcosm, govern successively these various time-periods are the 24 Elders, and they are identical with the 24 wings of the four Being.

The glassy sea is the ether specialized in the brain; the aura of the seven chakras being represented by the seven fire-lamps or Breaths.

The Master-God is Solar Man.

Ch. 4: 9-11

And as often as the Four Beings gave glory, honor, and thanks to the (Solar God) seated on the throne, to him who lives throughout the aeons of the aeons, the 24 Ancients kept falling down (successively) in front of the (Solar God) seated on the throne, worshipping him who lives throughout the aeons of the aeons, and letting fall their crowns in front of the throne, saying:

"Worthy thou art, our Master and our God, to receive the glory, the honor, and the force; for thou didst bring into existence the universe, and thru thy will it exists and was established."

INTERPRETATION

The forces preside in turn over the time-periods; thus in the human aura a tattva (principle or element) rules each hour, its particular psychic color predominating in the body's aura during that time. Hence the Ancients are represented as worshipping before the throne, each making obeisance in turn and casting down his crown, giving over his rule to the next.

CHAPTER NO. 19

Chap. 5: 1, 2

I saw on the right hand of the (Solar God) seated on the throne a scroll, written inside and on the back, sealed with seven seals. And I saw a strong Divinity proclaiming with a great voice:

"Who is worthy to open the scroll and force open its seals?"

INTERPRETATION

The scroll is a cosmic document which it has taken Cosmic Forces aeons to write, a Bible which, when rightly read, reveals cosmic mysteries.

The scroll is man's body; and its seven seals are the seven cells of the Vital Battery of the body. They are the same as the seven Societies and the seven little lampstands. The statement "written inside and on the back" refers to the cerebro-spinal and the great sympathetic nerve systems.

The "strong Divinity" is Kronos, the Father of Time, who in mythology is the oldest of the twelve great Gods.

Ch. 5: 3-5

No one--in the sky, on the earth, or under the earth--was able to open the scroll, or to see it.

I wept much because no worthy one was found to open the scroll or to see it. One of the Ancients says to Me:

"Do not weep. Behold! The Lion, he of the tribe of Juda, the root of David, has conquered: (he is worthy) to open the scroll and its seven seals."

INTERPRETATION

The Lion is, of course, Leo, a zodiacal sign, which is also the sign of Juda. The "root" of man is his solarical Self. For the Solar God, incarnated as man on earth, is the inverted ashvattha tree, which has its roots in the sky and its branches on the earth. So, "the root of David" is David reincarnated.

Ch. 5: 6, 7

I saw; and Behold! in the midst of the throne and the four Beasts, and in the midst of the Elders, there was a Lamb standing, as if it had been sacrificed, having seven horns and seven eyes, which are the seven Breaths of the God, sent off into all the earth. He came--he has taken (the scroll) from the right hand of (the God) seated on the throne.

INTERPRETATION

The Lamb is a variant of the zodiacal sign Ram, Aries; and the "Lamb" here is identical with the "Lion of the tribe of Juda," since the sign Leo is the sole domicile of the Sun, and Aries is the place of his highest exaltation.

Microcosmically, Leo corresponds to the sahasrara chakra, the Pineal gland, the "third eye," and Aries to the nimbus, or cerebral radiance.

This Lamb represents the incarnated Solar Man, which may be regarded as the Third Logos--man as he is on earth.

The horns and eyes are the seven noetic powers of action and the seven noetic perceptive faculties. Thus the Lamb represents the neophyte whose inner nature is awakening and who is about to undergo the perfecting, or initiatory, ordeals.

Ch. 5: 8-10

When he had taken the scroll, the four Beings and the 24 elders fell down in front of the Lamb, having each a lyre and a golden libation-saucer full of incense-offerings, which are the prayers of the devotees. And they changed a new lyric, saying:

"Worthy art thou to take the scroll and to open its seals; for thou wast sacrificed and didst buy for the God with thy blood (the good qualities) from every tribe, tongue, nation, and people, and didst make them (to be) a realm of sacrificers to our God; and they are ruling on the earth."

INTERPRETATION

Each of the elders has a discous cup used in pouring out drink-offerings to the Gods and also, like Apollo, a lyre.

The phiale (discous cup) symbolizes the chakra and the lyre the nerve-fibers connected with it.

Each chakra has its distinctive quality, color, sound, and incense-odor, all of which are perceivable by the psychic senses.

The four symbols used in the four conquests, the seal, the trumpet, the sickle, and the libation-saucer, appropriate represent the chakras also.

The neophyte is worthy to take control of the psychic mechanism of his own body, to "conquer" its chakras, tightening its slack organism till it is tense and vibrant as a lyre because he has in many incarnations, in every nation and in many conditions of life, acquired the nobler characteristics of each and moulded them into a character--a kingdom, truly--in which they are the ruling elements.

The chorus of praise by the four Beings and the 24 elders is the first of the seven choruses in the drama.

Ch. 5: 11-14

I saw; and I heard a voice of many Divinities around the throne: the Beasts and the elders--there were myriads of myriads--saying with a great voice:

"Worthy is the sacrificed Lamb to receive the force, wealth, skill, honor, glory, and praise.

Every existent being which is in the sky, on the earth, under the earth, and on the sea--the universe summed up in them--I heard saying:

"To the (God) seated on the throne, and to the Lamb, be the praise, the honor, the glory, and the dominion throughout the aeons of the aeons!"

And the four Beasts said "Amen." And the 24 elders fell down and worshipped (the God).

INTERPRETATION

The three peans chanted in praise of the Conqueror and his God are in accordance with the Greek custom of chanting peans to Apollo, the Sun God, before and after battle or before any solemn undertaking; and they are very appropriate here, as the Conqueror, the Lion-Lamb, represents the Solar Man, the microcosmic Sun, and having taken the scroll, he is about to undergo the ordeals of initiation. And the word Iesous, which is only a mystery name for Solar Man, has a most suspicious resemblance to Iesous, which is only a mystery name for Solar Man, has a most suspicious resemblance to Ieios, the epithet applied to Apollo because he was invoked in the peans by the reiterated cry "Ie," hailing him as the "Savior."

CHAPTER NO. 20

Ch. 6: 1-2

I saw, when the Lamb opened one of the seven seals, and I heard one of the four Beasts saying as with a voice of thunder: "Come!"

I saw; and, Behold! a white horse (came out). The (Divinity) who was riding him had a bow; to him was given a crown; and he came forth a conqueror and that he might keep on conquering.

INTERPRETATION

This seal is the Svadhishthana chakra, the prostatic, where the positive and negative currents of the Kundalini Force start. It corresponds to Sagittarius; hence its rider, the Bowman.

In this sign the Romans placed Diana, the Greek Letois, Apollo's sister, who was sometimes pictured as a bearded Goddess. Together they represent the male-female or androgynous man.

This chakra belongs to the lowest of the somatic divisions; yet, as the white horse, that division outranks the others, and the Bowman, Apollo-Diana, represents the Conqueror, who is here starting out on his conquests (of the chakras), and who reappears in triumph in the closing scene of the drama.

The Conqueror also corresponds to the human head of the sphinx (Aquarius-
-Waterman), which represents man as rising above his animalistic nature and reaching the throne gained in the resurrection (of the Pineal gland), where they neither marry nor are given in marriage, but are (free of lust) as the angels in heaven (Mat. 22:30).

Ch. 6: 3,4

When he opened the second seal, I heard the second Beast saying: "Come!"

Another horse, fiery-red, came out. To the (Divinity) who was riding him (authority) was given to take away peace from the earth--that (men) should slaughter one another--and to him was given a great sword.

INTERPRETATION

This seal is the Manipura chakra and its zodiacal sign in Scorpio, the house of Mars, the War-God.

Scorpio is usually given as corresponding to the generative centers; but the real seat of the epithumetic nature is the solar plexus.

The red horse represents the abdominal brain; and its rider, who is passion personified, appears later in the drama in the role of the Red Dragon.

Ch. 6: 5-6

When he opened the third seal, I heard the third Beast saying: "Come!"

I saw; and, Behold! a black horse (came out). The (Divinity) who was riding him had a balance in his hand. I heard as it were a voice in the midst of the four Beasts saying:

"A ration of wheat for a denarius and three rations of barley for a denarius --and do scant justice to the olive-oil and the wine."

INTERPRETATION

The thyroid-larynegeal chakra is the highest of those belonging strictly to the sympathetic nerve system, the ones above it being in the brain and belonging to the cerebro-spinal nerve system.

It is here presented as the regent of the highest of the somatic divisions, the "lower sky," for the cerebral region is termed in the Apocalypse the mid-sky, or zenith, as being the abode of the Solar God.

The vocal apparatus is, mystically, the creative organ of the Logos; and for this and other reasons, the white and the dun horses are given with their attributes interchanged.

The dun horse represents the lowest of the somatic divisions; and as sex exists only in the physical and psychic worlds, the two, Death and Hades, representing the generative principle on the two planes, are his riders, who slay with sword, famine, materialism, and animalism.

Ch. 6: 9-11

When he opened the fifth seal, I saw underneath the altar the souls of those who had been sacrificed because of the arcane doctrine of the God and because of the evidence which they had. They cried out with a great voice, saying:

"How long, O thou the Supreme, the Holy and True, dost thou fail to judge and avenge our blood upon those who dwell on the earth?"

White robes were given them severally, and it was said to them that they should keep still yet a little time, until their fellow slaves and also their brothers, who would be killed even as they were, should have finished (their course).

INTERPRETATION

The fifth seal here corresponds to the sign Cancer and the Ajna chakra, or cavernous plexus (Pituitary), the latter being closely connected with the Pituitary, the "membrum virile," so to say, of the brain.

The atrophied (sacrificed) brain-centers are partially aroused by the Serpentine Fire at this stage; but they are suppressed until the other centers (their brothers) have all been brought into action and then "killed," that is, placed in abeyance while the cerebral centers are being aroused. They receive "white robes," for at this center the positive and negative currents bifurcate, and their electrical emanations suffuse the brain.

During the cycle of reincarnation, all the chakras have been "slain" (dormantized) by the gross elements of the material, sensuous life; yet they retain the "evidence" of things solarical (previous activity).

While Leo precedes Cancer in the zodiacal signs, the order in which the chakras are activated is different; for Capricorn and Leo belong rather to the spinal than the sympathetic nerve system and are the two poles of the former.

Ch. 6: 12-17

I saw when he opened the sixth seal; and, Behold! there came to be a great earthquake; the sun became dark as a sack (woven of camel's) hair; the moon became as blood, and the stars of the sky fell to the earth, as a fig-tree drops her first crop of figs when shaken by a violent wind. The sky was removed like a scroll being rolled up; and every mountain and island--they were moved from their places. The rulers of the earth, the very great, the commanders, the rich and the mighty, and every slave and freeman, hid themselves in the caves and among the crags of the mountains; and they kept saying to the mountains and crags:

"Fall on us and hide us from the face of the (God) seated on the throne and from the passion of the Lamb. For the great day of his passion has come, and who can stand firm?"

INTERPRETATION

While this is the sixth seal here, this is the Muladhara chakra at the base of the spinal column, the point where the Sushumna nadi starts, and the starting point of the central current of the Serpentine Fire, the real Kundalini, the regenerative, redemptive force, here called the orge (fecundating force) of the "Lamb" (Solar Man).

This force rushes rapidly up to the brain; and upon the outpouring of this electric fire into the brain, the mind becomes blank, and the neophyte is conscious only of blind terror, allegorized as the darkening of the sun (mind); the falling of the stars (thoughts), the vanishing of the sky (concept of space), and the panic of the earth-dwellers (lower forces and faculties of the body.)

CHAPTER NO. 21

Ch. 7: 1-3

After these (ordeals) I saw four Divinities standing at the four corners of the earth, dominating the four winds of the earth so that no wind should blow on the earth or the sea, or on any tree. And I saw another (dominant) Divinity ascend from the birthplace of the sun, having the signet-ring of the living God; and he cried out with a great voice to the four Divinities to whom (authority) was given to punish the earth and the sea, saying:

"Do not punish the earth, the sea, or the trees till we shall have sealed (with his signet-ring) the slaves of our God on their foreheads."

INTERPRETATION

These five Divinities are the noetic regents of the Five Pranas, the Solar Life Winds. In Yoga literature they are termed the "divine energy of the Kundalini" and are manifested as Prana, Apana, Vyana, Samana, and Udana."

These five phases of the Solar Electricity of the air are represented in the Zodiac by the signs Gemini, Taurus, Aries, Pisces, and Aquarius, with their respective planets.

The four who guard the quarters are the four powers of Solar Man; and the fifth, who rises up from the sun's place of birth (anatole), is the representative of the Solar God himself and therefore bears the signet-ring of Life. They correspond to the "five bright powers" of the Upanishads, four of which are regents of the four directions of the compass, while the fifth "goes upward to immortality."

It is these noetic forces that record in the aura of man (his scroll of life) his every thought and deed; and, as these auric impressions, like phonographic records, automatically reproduce the original thoughts and emotions whenever the forces again act upon them, they thus produce an almost endless concatenation of cause and effect, of retributive action.

Therefore, by awakening the occult forces of his own self, the neophyte invokes this iron law of retribution; and all the good and evil elements of his nature are arrayed against each other for the final conflict.

In the Apocalyptic drama, the lower principles are to be chastized, and the higher ones are to be given the seal of the Solar God's approval.

Ch. 7: 4-8

I heard a number of those who were sealed, 144,000, sealed out of all the tribes of the children of Israel:

1. Of the tribe of Juda, 12,000
2. Of the tribe of Reuben, 12,000
3. Of the tribe of Gad, 12,000
4. Of the tribe of Asher, 12,000
5. Of the tribe of Naphtali, 12,000
6. Of the tribe of Simeon, 12,000
7. Of the tribe of Levi, 12,000
8. Of the tribe of Issachar, 12,000
9. Of the tribe of Zebulon, 12,000
10. Of the tribe of Manasseh, 12,000
11. Of the tribe of Joseph, 12,000
12. Of the tribe of Benjamin, 12,000

INTERPRETATION

These tribes represent the 12 signs of the Zodiac; Juda for Leo, Reuben for Aquarius, Gad for Aries, etc.; but as here listed by Apollonius, Joseph is substituted for Ephraim (Taurus); and Manasseh, Joseph's firstborn son, replaces Dan, who is Scorpio.

This omission of Dan, with the substitutions by which Scorpio is shown to be derived from Taurus, is significant; for Taurus is the symbol of the celestial creative force and Scorpio that of the generative function.

The Divinities charged with the seven scourges are, astronomically, the seven Pleiades, a star-group in the constellation of Taurus.

There was a Jewish tradition that from the tribe of Dan there was to come the Anti-Messias; hence the substitution of the paranatellon Aquila for Scorpio.

Ch. 7: 9-12

After these (things) I saw; and Behold! a vast multitude, which no one could count, from among every people, and of (all) tribes, nations, and tongues, (were) standing before the throne and before the Lamb, wearing white robes and (carrying) palm branches in their hands. They kept crying out with a great voice, saying:

"The deliverance is to the (Master) seated on the throne of our God, and to the Lamb!"

All the Divinities were standing in a circle about the throne, the elders and the four Beasts; they fell on their faces in front of the throne and worshipped the God, saying:

"Amen. The praise, the glory, the skill, the thanks, the honor, the force, and the strength be to our God throughout the aeons of the aeons! Amen."

INTERPRETATION

This is the third of the seven choruses of the drama; the verse, or pean of praise, is chanted by the liberated elements of the body, and the chorus by the ruling powers of the three worlds--the Beasts, Elders, and Divinities forming three concentric circles about the throne and thus representing as many planes of manifestation and also the Zodiac.

In the benediction, the attributes of all the seven planets are ascribed to the Solar God.

Ch. 7: 13-17

One of the elders responded, saying to me:

"These who are wearing the white robes--who are they, and whence did they come?"

I said to him: "My Master, you know."

He said to me:

"These are the (Conquerors) coming out of the great ordeal. They washed their robes and bleached them in the Lamb's blood. Because of this, they are before the throne of the God; and they are serving him day and night in his adytum, and the (Master) seated on the throne will spread his tent over them. They will hunger no more, thirst no more; neither will the sun beat down on them, nor any scorching heat. For the lamb, who is in the middle of the throne, will shepherd them and guide them to springs of waters of life, and the God will wipe away every tear from their eyes."

INTERPRETATION

The great ordeal of Solar Man is his incarceration in the carnal body, not merely for one short lifetime, but during the long series of incarnations throughout the aeons of generation.

But Solar Man has its own mighty purpose in thus crucifying itself by incarnating in the human form, descending into the spheres of generation and passing thru the vast "cycle of necessity": For it builds up for itself, out of the elements of the lower worlds, an outer self, a being formed of the "dust of the earth," the refuse of past cycles; and then by unremitting toil throughout the aeons it refines and transmutes the elements of this being (who is the carnal), animal-human man) until it redeems it, and it becomes one with the divine individuality.

These purged and redeemed principles of the lower self are the countless host who, now that the aspirant has entered upon the cycle of initiation, the final "perfecting" labor, are coming out of "the great ordeal," singing peans of praise to the sacrificial Lamb, the Crucified, and to the enthroned Self, the Eternal, the Solar Man, who is beyond change and time and therefore "uncrucified."

CHAPTER NO. 22

Ch. 8: 1-6

When he opened the seventh seal, there came to be silence in the sky for about half an hour.

I saw the seven Divinities who stand before the God. To them were given seven trumpets. Came another Divinity and stationed himself above the altar, having a golden censer; and to him was given much incense, that he might offer it, with the prayers of all the devotees, upon the golden altar in front of the throne. The smoke of the incense, with the prayers of the devotees, went up in front of the God out of the Divinity's hand. The Divinity took the censer and filled it with the fire of the altar, and cast (it) into the earth: There came to be voices, thunders, lightnings and an earthquake. The seven Divinities having the seven trumpets made themselves ready to give the trumpet calls.

INTERPRETATION

The seventh seal is the Sahasrara chakra, to which corresponds the zodiacal sign Leo, the sole domicile of the Sun.

This chakra, the Pineal gland, is the third eye of the Seer--that, and much more. It is the focal point of all the forces of the nerve system and of the aura. Here they come to an equilibrium and here reigns the mystic Silence.

During the meditation, as each chakra is activated, the neophyte is able to see its corresponding psychic color; and at this seventh center, the colors blend as in an opal, with an incessant glittering of white light playing as on the facets of a diamond.

The psychic senses of smell and hearing begin to be awakened, so that odors, as of incense, become perceptible, and mysterious sounds are heard. Then with a shock, which Apollonius here compares to an earthquake, the Kundalini Force starts upon the circuit of the seven brain-centers, each of which, when the current reaches it, produces a vibrant sound in the aura, allegorized as a "trumpet call." So there are seven trumpets to match the seven brain-centers.

The Divinity who stationed himself above the altar, having a golden censer, is the Hierophant or the Initiator.

Ch. 8:7

The first (Divinity) gave the trumpet-call. There came to be hail and fire, mixed with blood; they were cast into the earth, and a third of the earth was burnt up, and all fresh grass was burnt.

INTERPRETATION

Of the four planes of consciousness, the fourth, the physical, was stilled, or temporarily suppressed, by the opening of the seals, and the psychic became active. Now, by the activation of the noetic centers, the psychic consciousness, "the third," is in turn placed in abeyance.

The colors manifested by the centers of the sympathetic nerve system are psychic; and the sounds heard upon the activation of the brain-centers pertain to a higher plane.

The "hail" is a semi-condensation of the lunar element, or ether, "the cooling water of the Moon," the Ida nadi; the "fire" is the solar force of the Pingala nadi, "the golden fire of the Sun"; and the "blood" is the red auric fluid, called "the blood of the Logos."

These three elements affect the lowest of the somatic divisions; the "trees" are the "two olive-trees", the dual tree of life, the Ida and Pingala nadis, and the "grass" is the radiation of the same force through the aureola. They are, of course, the threefold Serpentine Fire, starting on its course thru the brain.

Ch. 8: 8, 9

The second Divinity gave the trumpet-call. (It was) as if a great flaming mountain of fire was cast into the sea; and a third of the sea turned to blood. The third of the existent beings in the sea, having souls, died; and a third of the ships were wrecked.

INTERPRETATION

This is the activation of the Manipura chakra in the solar plexus area, and the active volcano is a symbol of Mars, the planetary force ruling the epithumetic nature, "the sea."

Ch. 8: 10, 11

The third Divinity gave the trumpet-call. There fell from the sky a great star flaming as a torch. It fell on the third of the rivers and on the springs of waters. The name of the star is called Wormwood; and a third of the waters became wormwood, and many of the men died of the waters, because they were made bitter.

INTERPRETATION

The falling star is Aphrodite (Venus), the torch-bearing Goddess, and also "the Devata Isha who is connected with Siva."

The force it here symbolizes affects the emotional psychic nature; and meditation on this area, the Anahata chakra, "gives one the power to protect and destroy worlds." It also makes one wise and full of noble deeds; and "the Yogi who concentrates his mind in Anahata becomes dearer than the dearest to the women; but he must resist them. So, the imbittering of the waters alludes to the psychological law that all pleasure eventually reacts and becomes pain; yet, in the end, this bitter water of self-denial becomes transmuted into the "sweet water of life."

Ch. 8: 12

The Fourth Divinity gave the trumpet call. The third of the sun was stricken, and also the third of the moon and the third of the stars, so that the third of them should be darkened, and the day should not give light for the third of it, and likewise the night.

INTERPRETATION

This is the Vishuddha chakra, the Thyroid area. All mental action is here suspended on the psychic, or subjective, plane, as well as on the material or objective. On each plane, in turn, the forces have to be brought into equilibrium, so that they neutralize each other, and then the consciousness rises to the next higher plane.

The adept, by much meditation on this chakra, becomes exceedingly wise and enjoys constant mental peace. "He can destroy all dangers and see the past, present and future. Such a one is able to move the three worlds and his power, if he chose to use it, could not be restrained even by Brahma."

Ch. 8:13

I saw; and I heard a lone Eagle, flying in midsky, saying with a great voice:

"Woe, woe, woe to those dwelling on the earth, from the remaining trumpet-voices of the three Divinities who are about to give the trumpet-call."

INTERPRETATION

As already indicated, the earth man is an inverted image of the solar man; and from this it follows that the highest solarical centers are directly related to the lowest, the creative centers on the material plane.

For this reason the three trumpet-calls are announced as "woes" by the eagle, the fourth of the Zoa, who is the prototype of Scorpio.

It cannot be too emphatically reiterated that sexual generation exists only in the physical and psychic worlds.

All of the ancient philosophy revolved round this mysterious world of creation in the human body, which has been so sorely disgraced by abuse and misuse that no one dares to talk about it now--that world of creation in the body.

The abuse of this function is the most terrible of all crimes, the "blasphemy against the Holy Pnerma," and the "unpardonable sin"--the punishment of which by natural law is the annihilation of the individuality, the second death."

It is only the celibates who preserve the utmost purity of mind and body, thereby preserving the complete innocence of "little children," who can hope to "enter the kingdom of heaven."

CHAPTER NO. 23

Ch. 9: 1-12

The fifth Divinity gave the trumpet-call. I saw a star that has fallen from the sky to the earth; and to him was given the key to the crater of the abyss. He opened the crater, and there went up smoke, like the smoke of a furnace. The sun and air were darkened by the smoke. Out of the smoke came locusts upon the earth, and to them was given license as the scorpions of the earth have license. It was said to them that they should not punish the grass of the earth, neither saying tender-green nor any tree, but only those men who do not have the seal of the God on their foreheads; and (the command) was given them that they should not kill them, but that they should be tormented five months. Their torment was as a scorpion's torment when it stings a man.

In those days men will seek death and find it not; they will long to die, and death will keep fleeing from them.

The effigies of the locusts were like horses caparisoned for battle. On their heads were (circlets) like crowns of spurious gold. Their faces were like men's faces, but they had hair like women's hair; and their teeth were like the teeth of lions. They had cuirasses like iron cuirasses. The voice of their wings was like the voice of war-chariots, of many horses galloping into battle. They have tails like scorpions, and stings were in their tails. Their license to punish men was five months. They have over them as ruler the Divinity of the Abyss; his name in Hebrew is Abaddon, and in the Greek (mysticism) he has the name Apollyon.

The one woe has passed. Behold! two more woes are coming after.

INTERPRETATION

The star that has fallen is Venus, now becomes the so-called "infernal Lucifer," the Hecate who presides over the abyss.

This abyss is represented astronomically by the constellation Crater, the Cup, the mixing-bowl of Iacchos, the phallic God. It appears in the Apocalypse as the cup held by the Woman in scarlet, who is simply Hecate, the infernal aspect of both Aphrodite (Venus) and Letois (Diana), the two Goddesses alike symbolizing the primordial substance, the Arch.

The Divinity of the Abyss, who is the "Destroyer" and the "Murderer," is the Pseudo-Lion, the Beast--the phrenic mind polluted by the carnal passions; and his hordes of scorpion-like cavalry are low and impure thoughts.

The "five months" represent the summertime, during which period the passional nature is more active. Mystically, the summer is said to be the night of Solar Man, and winter, his day.

Ch. 9: 13-15

The sixth Divinity gave the trumpet-call. I heard a single voice from the four horns of the golden altar in front of the God (the master's voice), saying to the sixth Divinity, who had the trumpet:

"Turn loose the four Divinities who are fettered at the great river Euphrates."

The four Divinities were turned loose who had been made ready throughout the hour, day, month and year, that they should kill the third of man.

INTERPRETATION

Here the golden altar is the Nous, or higher mind, and the four horns are its four powers. Gold is the metal of the sun (condensed sun-rays), and the four-horned altar is but a different symbol for the sun and the regents of the four quarters. The four Divinities fettered at the Euphrates (cerebro-spinal cord) are the pranas, life-winds. The Nous and the four Divinities are the analogues, on the purely intellectual plane, of the Logos and the four Zoa.

Ch. 9: 16-21

The number of the armies of the horsemen (under the command of the four Divinities) was two hundred million--I heard the number of them.

Thus I saw the horses in the vision, and their riders, having cuirasses fiery (red), smoke blue and sulphurous (yellow); the heads of the horses were like the heads of lions; and from their mouths keep going out fire, smoke, and sulphur. By these three scourges were killed the third of the men--by the fire, smoke, and sulphur which went out of their mouths.

For the powers of the horses are in their mouths, and in their tails; for their tails are like snakes and have heads, and with them they inflict punishment.

The rest of the men, who were not killed by these scourges, did not reform from the works of their hands, that they should not worship the spirits and the images of gold, silver, bronze, stone and wood, which can neither see, hear, nor walk. And they did not reform from their murders, their sorceries, their prostitutions or their thefts.

INTERPRETATION

The armies of horsemen represent the limitless powers of the Nous; the lion-heads of the horses indicating the solar character.

As Mind is the real man, so in the allegory the intellectual powers and thoughts are represented as men, the armies of the Mind destroying the evil, false, superstitious thoughts and tendencies of the psychic nature. And as the thoughts of the Carnal Mind are concerned largely with material possessions, such thoughts are referred to as worshippers of idols.

CHAPTER NO. 24

Ch. 10: 1-4

I saw another, (the) strong Divinity, coming down out of the sky, wrapped in a cloud, and a rainbow was upon his head. His face was like the sun, and his feet like pillars of fire. In his hand he had a scroll unrolled. He placed his right foot on the sea, and the left on the earth, and cried out with a great voice, as a lion roars; and when he cried out, seven thunders uttered voices of their own. And I was about to write down (the teachings); but I heard a voice from the sky saying to me:

"Seal up (the teachings) which the seven thunders uttered, and do not write them down."

INTERPRETATION

The strong Divinity is the fifth in the group, the Nous, the intellectual Sun, in its aspect as Kronos, old Father Time.

This fivefold group is the same as that which appeared at the opening of the sixth seal, save that here they are energizing on a higher plane.

That the voices of the seven thunders were mystery-teachings is indicated by the injunction of the Initiator against recording them. They were for the Initiates only and not for the multitude.

Ch. 10: 5-7

The Divinity whom I saw standing on the sea and on the earth raised his right hand to the sky and swore by the (God) who lives throughout the aeons of the aeons, who brought into existence the sky and what is in it, the earth and what is in it, and the sea and what is in it, that Time shall be no more, but in the days of the voice of the Seventh Divinity, when he is about to give the trumpet-call, also shall be made perfect the Mystery of the God, as he proclaimed to his slaves, the seers.

INTERPRETATION

Time, the "image of eternity," rules in the physical and psychic realms, symbolized in the allegory as the earth and the sea. But in the spiritual (electrical) world, the mystic "sky," there prevails the timeless, limitless, eternal consciousness of the Solar God.

The seventh trumpet-call signalized the opening (activation) of that "Mystery of the God," the Pineal Gland, the single eye of the Seer, made perfect, resurrected from its dormant state and restored to its solarical and electrical functions by the action of the ascending Kundalini Force.

*** *** *** *** ***

In these seven trumpet-calls, we have again traced the ascent of the Kundalini Force up thru the chakras to the Pineal gland in the brain, the abode of Siva, who is eternal. Now we enter into another phase of the subject.

Ch. 10: 8-11

The voice that I heard from the sky (I heard it) again speaking to me and saying:

"Go, take the little scroll unrolled in the hand of the Divinity who is standing on the sea and on the earth."

I went to the Divinity, asking him to give me the little scroll. He says to me:

"Take it, and eat it. It will make your belly bitter; but in your mouth it will be sweet as honey."

I took the little scroll and ate it. In my mouth it was as honey sweet; but when I had eaten it, my belly was made bitter, and (the voices of the seven thunders) keep saying to me:

"You must teach again in opposition to many nations, peoples, tongues, and rulers."

INTERPRETATION

The little scroll is the secret arcane science handed down from times immemorial. Its teachings are --

He that overcometh the desires of the flesh and the passions of the blood, and obeyeth the commandment not to eat of the "forbidden fruit," the same shall inherit all things good in life; and I, Perfection, will be his Guide, and he shall be my Son.

When these teachings are carried out in practice, they become "bitter" to the epithumetic nature, since they inculcate the extirpation of every impure thought and lustful desire. And the reaction that follows is "sweet as honey" to Solar Man.

Although forbidden to record the utterances of the seven thunders (the theurgic teachings), the Seer is under an obligation to proclaim to all people the true philosophy and ethics of the Higher Life in opposition to the popular dogmas of the exoteric religions. And his reward for so doing will be his banishment to darkness "for the good of the people."

CHAPTER NO. 25

Ch. 11: 1-3

There was given me a reed like a wand, (the first voice) saying:

"Rise up, and measure the adytum of the God, the altar, and those worshipping in it; but the court which is exterior to the adytum cast out as exoteric, and do not measure it; for it has been given to the people, and the holy city they shall trample on for forty-two months. I shall give it (after that) to my two witnesses, and they will teach one thousand two hundred and sixty days, clothed in gunny-sacks."

INTERPRETATION

The adytum was the inner temple, or sanctuary, where the God was enshrined and to which none had access but the initiated. When used for initiatory rites, it was usually called the adytum.

Symbolically, the adytum is the psychic nature, and the altar the intellectual. Astronomically, it is the sky. But in the psycho-physiological rendering of the symbolism, the adytum, the altar of sacrifice and the altar of incense are the three divisions of the brain, the cerebrum, cerebellum and medulle oblongata, and the outer court is the physical body.

The worshippers are the forty-nine forces, which are "measured" by being arranged in hierarchies, or groups.

Here the period of initiation is placed at seven years, during the first half of which the lower forces continue to rule the functions of the body, while in the latter half (three and one-half years), the dual electric forces, the Ida and Pingala nadis, the "two witnesses," will pervade the nerve system, gradually and almost imperceptibly replacing the ordinary, lower-grade nerve force--a subdued action which is expressed in the allegory by their being wrapped in gunny-sacks.

The measuring of the adytum and the account of the two witnesses have nothing to do with the action of the drama, being merely explanatory.

Ch. 11: 4-6

These are the two olive-trees, and two little lampstands, standing before the God of the earth. If any one wills to use them wrongfully, fire comes out of their mouth and devours their enemies; and if any one shall will to use them wrongfully, in this way must he be killed.

These (two witnesses) have authority to shut the sky, so that rain may not shower down during the days of their teaching; also they have authority over the waters, to transmute them into blood, and to chastise the earth with every scourge, as often as they may will.

INTERPRETATION

In the 4th chapter of the Zechariah are given more details concerning the two olive-trees and lampstands, reference to which we have previously made.

In the Zechariah it is written:

"I have seen; and Behold! a candlestick all of gold, with a bowl upon the top of it, and its seven lamps thereon; and there are seven pipes to each of the lamps, which are upon the top thereof; and two olive-trees by it, one upon the right side of the bowl, and one upon the left side thereof" (Zech. 4: 2,3).

The candlestick is the spine, the bowl is the skull, the seven lamps are the seven chakras and their nadis, and the two olive-trees are the Ida and Pingala nadis. As they are small and seemingly unimportant, the ancient scribe continued:

"For who hath despised the day of small things? For they (the seven) shall rejoice and shall see the plummet in the hand of Zerubbabel, even these seven (which are) the eyes of Jehovah; they run to and fro through the whole earth" (human body) (Zech. 4:10).

We have said that Zerubbabel represents the Pituitary gland in the brain, and when stimulated by the ascending Creative Fire, its pulsating aura increases and assumes a swaying movement, like a plummet, until the force impinges on the Pineal gland, later explained more in detail, impregnating that gland with the golden force and stimulating it into mysterious activity, as we shall later notice.

This physiological process, unknown to modern science, is further described in the Zechariah, which says, "the two olive-trees" and "the two olive branches which are beside the two golden spouts, that empty the golden (oil) out of themselves" are "the two anointed ones (Ida and Pingala nadis) that stand by the Lord (Solar Man) of the whole earth" (Zech. 4:11-14).

The electric fire that flows thru the Ida and Pingala nadis is destructive to the unpurified psychic or sorcerer who may succeed in arousing it and yet is unprepared for the event. Its wrongful use results in moral as well as physical death.

By "rain" the nerve fluid is symbolized; "water" is the magnetic, auric substance, and "blood" is the glowing electric fire. The "chastisement" of the earth is later described in the drama as the pouring out of seven scourges by the seven Taurine Divinities, the Pleiades.

Ch. 11: 7

When they shall have finished giving their evidence, the Beast who comes up out of the abyss will battle with them, conquer them, and kill them.

INTERPRETATION

According to the Hindu Masters, when the trance is ended, and the neophyte returns to the common state of consciousness on the material plane, the Kundalini Force recedes to the "throne of the Beast," the solar plexus region, where it is said in the Upanishads to lie coiled up like a slumbering serpent, having three and a half coils, corresponding to the three-and-a-half measures of the AUM. All of which, no doubt, is Hindu nonsense, but to which we must adhere in this interpretation of the allegory.

Ch. 11: 8,9

Their corpses (are now lying) in the main-street of the great city which is mystically called "Sodom" and "Egypt," where also their Master was crucified. And (some) from among the nations, tribes, tongues and people are guarding their corpses three-and-a-half days, and will not permit their dead bodies to be placed in a sepulchre.

INTERPRETATION

The city is the body, and its main-street is the spinal column, in which are the channels of the threefold Serpentine Fire, consisting of the Sushumna; Ida and Pingala nadis, the witnesses, and their Masters, Solar Man, "who was crucified."

These three channels, the "corpses" of the witnesses, are preserved from complete atrophy by the nerve forces which, in each of the four divisions of the body, flows thru the cerebro-spinal system.

The three-and-a-half days are the latter half of the seven "days of Creation" mentioned in the Bible, the gross material ARC of the cycle of human evolution, during which the "witnesses" lie moribund in the mystical "Sodom."

The formula "nations, tribes, tongues and people" is given seven times in the drama, but the words are never twice in the same order; in one instance (10:11) "rulers" is substituted for "tribes," and in another (17:15) "multitude" for the same. They apply to the four castes, or classes of mankind, who in Hindu mysticism are said to have been born of the four somatic divisions of "Deity"; men of learning, warriors, laborers, and commercialists.

Iesous (Solar Man) is said to have been crucified in Sodom, also called Egypt. This is the first crucifixion and refers to the incarnation of Solar Man in the physical body, which then becomes the Cross of physical existence.

Man hangs on the Cross as he clings to the passions and pleasures of his material body, with its qualities of sensations and emotions.

The body, and everything connected with it in a material, sensual, animalistic way, is called the "vail." This Vail blinds us to the real Man and causes us to think that our earthly body and earthly life are all there is.

This "vail of the temple" (body) is the illusion that "was rent in twain from the top to the bottom" when the gospel Jesus was crucified (Mat. 27:51).

When terrestrial man is killed or crucified, then Celestial Man comes forth (born again), freed from his physical prison, and is presented in the drama as that "great city, the new Jerusalem, descending out of heaven" (Rev. 21:10).

Another version of the same parable is presented in the case of the prodigal son who took a trip to a far country and learned by painful experience that earthly life is all ashes, aches, vanity, and illusion. But it is a necessary school of experience; and once we escape from earthly existence, we shall never want to take the trip again, where every pleasure and joy turn in the end to pain and disappointment.

This is the earthly life to which the Masters referred when they said, "Cursed is every man that hangeth on a tree" (Deut. 21:23; Gal. 3:13).

Solar Man comes forth in all his glory when he sheds the material garment and realizes that he is really "one with the Father" (Jn. 10:30), the Great Solar Orb, the Father of all, the same as all light is one with electricity.

The light of an electric globe is the identical light that comes from the power plant. The light in the globe is not separate from the electricity in the power plant, the Father of light. They are both one and the same. And so each one of us is a Spark of the Great Solar Orb, as explained in our work titled "ANCIENT SUN GOD."

Ch. 11:10-4

Those who dwell on the earth are rejoicing over them and are exultant; and they will send bribes to one another, for those two seers did torment those who are dwelling on the earth.

After the three-and-a-half days the Breath of Life from the God entered into them, they stood on their feet; and great terror overcame those who beheld them. They heard a great voice from the sky saying to them:

"Come up hither."

They went up into the sky in the cloud; and their enemies beheld them. In that hour there came to be a great earthquake, and the tenth of the city fell; and there were killed by the earthquake the names of men seven thousand; the rest became frightened and gave glory to the God of the sky.

The second woe has passed. Behold! the third woe is coming speedily.

INTERPRETATION

The rebuking voice of conscience, which is the voice of Solar Man speaking thru the "two witnesses," is the real tormentor of the evilly disposed who seek ever to stifle that voice. And the man who is thus trying to silence his accusing conscience cannot be mentally honest with himself, but acts from feigned motives, his desires, and thoughts, bribing one another, as the allegory phrases it. But as the individual emerges from the materialistic stage of his evolution, the noetic faculties "awaken from the dead," and the base passional nature, symbolized by the tenth of the twelve zodiacal divisions, perishes with its seven heads, for it is identified with the seven-headed red Dragon.

The seven is multiplied by the indefinite number one thousand to indicate the many correlations of these lower principles, the "men" whose "names" are their psychic colors, which are obliterated, the remaining colors becoming brighter in the auric "glory" of the Solar God.

Ch. 11: 15-18

The seventh Divinity gave the trumpet-call. There came to be great voices in the sky saying:

"The realm of the world has become that of our Master and of his Anointed, and he shall reign throughout the aeons of the aeons."

The 24 elders who are seated before the God on their thrones fell on their faces and worshipped the God, saying:

"We give thanks to thee, the Master-God, the All-Dominator who (forever) art, and who wast, because thou hast taken thy great force and regained sovereignty. The people grew passionate; and thy passion came, and the season of the dead to be judged and (the season) to give their recompense to thy slaves the seers, to the devotees, and to those who fear thy name, the small and the great, and to destroy those who are destroying the earth."

INTERPRETATION

The seventh of the mystic "psychic sounds" signalizes the activation of the Sahasrara chakra, situated in the crown of the head, "the dwelling place of Siva," the center thru which radiates the Light of the Logos.

The passion of the Solar God is not his "wrath," but the creative energy of the Logos, the "great force" that produces the "birth from above"; and it is here placed in contrast with the passions of man's animalistic nature that "are destroying the earth."

The chorus by the sky-voices and the elders is the fourth of the series.

Ch. 11: 19

The adytum of the God in the sky was opened (activated), and in his adytum was seen the ark (containing the emblems) of his compact; and there came to be lightnings, voices, thunders, an earthquake, and great hail.

INTERPRETATION

The constellation Arca, the celestial Ship, situated to the south of Virgo, was also called "Noah's Ark."

As the exoteric exponents of phallicism are fond of pointing out, the Ark is a symbol of the female womb, the place of birth--which is literally true if regarded as merely a concrete symbol.

But esoterically, it has no such phallic significance, as it represents the exact opposite, the place of Solarical, Electrical Rebirth, the emergence into immortality. It symbolizes the Womb in the brain, the latter being an androgynous organ wherein is immaculately conceived the permanent vehicle, the solar body, according to Hindu philosophy.

CHAPTER NO. 26

Ch. 12: 1, 2

A great constellation was seen in the sky: a (winged) Woman clothed with the sun, the moon under her feet, and on her head a crown of twelve stars. She had (a babe) in her womb, and she keeps crying out, in the pangs of childbirth, raked with the pain of parturition.

INTERPRETATION

The seventh trumpet-call is the sound heard when the Pineal gland is activated, and it corresponds to the sign Leo, the house of the Sun. But the constellation here presented is triadic, including in the symbol the signs Virgo (house of Mercury), Leo, and Cancer (domicile of the Moon).

Thus associated, Virgo is the Virgin Mother who immaculately conceives and gives birth to the Son of the God; whereas, taken in combination with Libra (house of Venus) and Scorpio (house of Mars), she becomes the scarlet prostitute, the symbol of animalistic generation.

As the World Mother, the White Virgin of the Skies, whether called Isis, Diana, or Aphrodite, is the Pure Ether, the Logos Light, the Primordial Force Substance, the Refined Solar Electricity. And as the Fallen Woman, the Queen of the Abyss, she is the parturient energy of nature, the basis of physical life; and as such she is named in the Apocalypse Sodom, Babylon, and Egypt, merely to make her threefold like her celestial prototype, for in reality she includes all cities and countries inhabited by sinful mankind.

Virgo was always pictured with wings in ancient scriptures; and later in the text she has the two wings of the Eagle.

In this case, in simpler terms, Woman represents the World Mother; the sun and moon represent the male and female principles of production and the crown of twelve months of the year and also the twelve signs of the Zodiac.

As sunshine on the earth makes the earth produce, so in this symbolism the sun shines on Woman, and she produces. While ancient symbolism may not always be precise in detail, it always illustrates cosmic principles in action.

Ch. 12: 3-6

Another constellation was seen in the sky--and, Behold! a great red Dragon, having seven heads and ten horns and on his head seven diadems. His tail was trailing along the third of the stars of the sky and kept throwing them to the earth.

The Dragon was standing in front of the Woman who was on the verge of parturition, so that as soon as she gave birth he might devour her child. She gave birth to a son, virile, who is destined to shepherd all the people with an iron wand; and her child was snatched up to the God and to this throne. The Woman fled into the desert, where she has a place made ready by the God, that there (the Divinities) may nourish her one thousand two hundred and sixty days.

INTERPRETATION

In connection with this, the student should read our work titled THE GREAT RED DRAGON (61 8½ x 11 pgs. ills. cover - $3.50 from Health Research).

This constellatory symbol is Draco, the pole Dragon, which has seven distinguishing stars and which, as depicted in ancient star-maps, extends over seven of the zodiacal signs and, in setting, apparently sweeps a third of the starry sky down to the horizon.

Microcosmically it symbolizes the passional nature, epithumia, the Apocalyptic number of which is 555.

The energizing of the cerebral centers produces a reflex action in the lower nature; and unless the neophyte is duly purified, the Dragon will indeed devour the child, not at the time of its birth, but at the moment of conception. For according to Hindu philosophy, the Solar Body is not born at this time, but only has its inception, though the psychic form may be projected.

Hindu philosophy taught that the Real Man "is neither born, nor doth it die. Unborn, undying ancient, perpetual, and eternal, it hath endured and will endure forever." (Bhagavad Gita, p. 27).

In the Ancient Greek Mysteries, this stage of the initiatory work was represented quite badly as the generative act; but Apollonius has handled the subject more delicately, by substituting for the solar the psychic body, which is "born" with the physical body and develops conjointly with it.

According to the allegory, the Conqueror is not born until after three-and-a-half years (1260 days), during which time the Woman is being nourished by the Divinities; and the statement that the child is caught up to the throne connotes "a period of spiritual gestation," according to Hindu philosophy.

The immaculate conception is here represented by the opening of the adytum and disclosure of the Ark. Those who have investigated the subject of the Ark know that the emblems it contained are the genitals.

Ch. 12: 7-12

There came to be a battle in the sky. Mikael and his Divinities gave battle to the Dragon; and the Dragon and his Divinities gave battle, but they lacked strength, nor was their place found in the sky anymore.

Hurled down was the great Dragon, the archaic Snake, who is called the "Accuser" and the "Adversary," the deluder of the whole earth; he was hurled down to the earth, and his Divinities were hurled down with him. I heard a great voice in the sky saying:

"Now are attained the deliverance, the force, and the ruling of our God and the authority of his Anointed. For hurled down is the prosecutor of our brothers, who keeps prosecuting them before our God day and night. But they conquered him through the blood of the Lamb and through the arcane doctrine of his evidence; and they did not esteem their psychic bodies until death.

"Therefore rejoice, ye skies, and ye who are pitching tent in them; (but) woe to the earth and the sea--for the Accuser has gone down to you having great lust, knowing that he has but a short season."

INTERPRETATION

The battle between Mikael and the Dragon, with their respective hordes, resulting in the expulsion of the Evil (Black) Serpent from the sky, means the exclusion from the Mind of all impure thoughts, especially those relating to carnal lust.

The Dragon represents the principle of Desire in all its innumerable gradations, from the vaguest yearnings and the mere promptings of the appetites of the body down to the grossest phases of passion and lust; and all of these have their source in the powerful instinct of reproduction, the attracting and cohering force of generated life. "The deluder of the whole earth" is an excellent expression, for carnal lust is the curse of mankind.

The creative Logos is the Dragon of Light; and its opposite is the Dragon of Darkness, the deluder of the whole people of the earth who is conquered "thru the blood of the Lamb," which means the sacrification of his animalistic nature by his obligation of initiation.

They did not esteem their psychic bodies until death means that the psychic body is chiefly of importance after physical demise.

Ch. 12: 13-17

When the Dragon saw that he was cast down to the earth, he kept pursuing the Woman who gave birth to a male child. The Woman was endowed with the Eagle's wings so that she might fly to the desert, to her place, where she is being nourished for a season and seasons and half a season from the face of the Snake.

The Snake spouted water after the Woman, like a river, that he might cause her to be carried away by the torrent. The earth rescued the Woman; the earth opened her mouth and swallowed the river. The Dragon waxed passionate over the Woman and went away to battle with the rest of her seed, who keep the commands of the God and have the evidence of the Anointed Iesous; and he stationed himself on the sand of the sea.

INTERPRETATION

The Virgin Mother is here the Sushumna nadi; the two wings of the Eagle are the Ida and Pingala nadis. The Winged woman represents the objective, or substantial, working of the Kundalini Force, while the three witnesses answer to its subjective, or noetic, aspect.

Foiled in his designs on the male child (nascent solar body), the Dragon seeks to arrest the psychical growth of the neophyte by pouring out a flood of psychic phenomenal illusions; but the force thus engendered is absorbed by material nature; and then, stationing himself on the margin of the sea (the finer and more esthetic elements of the epithumetic principle), he combats the intuitions of the intellectual nature.

Astronomically, the river spouted out by the Dragon is Eridanus, a winding constellation in the southern hemisphere, also called the River of Orion, which, when Virgo is in ascension, is setting and therefore apparently being swallowed by the earth.

The phrase "season and seasons and half a season," is a puzzling variant of the 42 months and the 1260 days, or three-and-a-half years.

CHAPTER NO. 27

Ch. 13: 1-4

I saw rising out of the sea a (constellatory) Beast, having ten horns and seven heads, and on his horns, ten diadems, and on his heads (seven) names of profanities.

The Beast was like a leopard, his feet were like a bear's; and his mouth was like a lion's. The Dragon gave him his force and his throne and great authority. I saw one of his heads (drooping) as if it had been slain in the Death (-world); but his death-blow was healed.

The whole earth became admiring followers of the Beast. They also worshipped the Dragon because he gave authority to the Beast, and they worshipped the Beast, saying:

"Who is a match for the Beast? Is any one strong enough to meet him in combat?"

INTERPRETATION

In steliar symbolism, the Beast is the constellation now called Cetus, which is represented not as a Whale but as a nondescript marine monster. The Arabians and the Jews called it the Sea-Lion; and it was also named the Leopard and the Sea-Bear. Apollonius has combined these various representations of it, presenting a composite picture.

As a caricature of the psycho-physical mind, the original figure, in the form drawn by those who invented the zodiacal language, would seem to be sufficiently grotesque; but Apollonius has given it additional touches of satire.

The Beast is said to rise from the sea and to receive power from the Dragon because it is the product of the two lower levels, the psychic and the physical. Its seven heads are the seven ruling epithumetic desires, each of which is a profanation of the Divine Desire. Its ten horns are the five intellectual faculties doubled because its every faculty is dual and at war with itself. The horns are all adorned with diadems to indicate the false pride of the lower intellect. As the lower mind is the shadow of the true mind, the Nous, which is symbolized as the Lion, the Beast is pictured as a Pseudo-Lion, a hybrid, as it resembles the Leopard, which was fabled to be a cross between the Lion (Leo) and the Panther (pardus); it is slow-going, with the ponderous waves of the Bear and has a mouth like a Lion, thus stimulating the voice of the Nous. It represents the highest development of man's intellect dissociated from philosophic reason and psychic intuition, and it is indeed the admiration of the world of the profane.

The head that is seemingly slain and yet resurrects is the desire for life on the plane of the physical senses, a desire which the neophyte must utterly eradicate.

In a more general sense, the lower mind, whenever it attempts philosophy, is never quite sure that life is worth living if all sensuality must be discarded; and in its utter blindness to higher realities, perceiving only the phenomena of the physical world, it formulates theories of existence based entirely on them, regarding all else as unknowable and unworthy of effort.

Ch. 13: 5-10

There was given him a mouth speaking great (boastings) and profanities; and authority was given him to do (this) for 42 months. He opened his mouth in profanity against the God, to profane his name, his tent, and those pitching tent in the sky. It was given him to do battle with the devotees and to conquer them; and authority was given him over every tribe, nation, tongue, and people. All those who dwell on the earth will worship him--(every one) whose name has not been registered in the sacrificed Lamb's scroll of life since the evolution of the world.

If any one has an ear, let him hear: If any one welcomes captivity, into captivity he goes; if any one shall kill with the sword, with the sword must he be killed. Here is the patience and the faith of the devotees.

INTERPRETATION

In this allegorical exposition of the powers and peculiarities of the lower mind-principle, only part applies to the Conqueror, the best being of a general nature. For without this broader application, the treatment of the subject would be incomplete and obscure.

The 42 months refers to the first half of the seven-year initiatory cycle, during which the neophyte, passing thru the psychic stages of his development, and thereby intensifying the action of the psycho-phrenic mind, must struggle constantly against its influence; but the rest of the explanatory matter relates to humanity in general.

Those who have not been registered in the Book of Life (see also ch. 17:8) are the great majority who have not in any incarnation, during the cycle of physical evolution, attained the noetic consciousness.

For, once a man has even glimpsed the supernal truths, he enters a new world and can never again rest content with the illusory images of the material world, or worship at the shrine of mere intellectualism. The true Self, the Master-Mind, has placed his seal upon him; and he is thenceforth individualized from the irresponsible mass of mankind and enrolled among those who must, by an irresistible impulse (the call of the God), tread the Royal Path of Man's Higher Destiny.

The word "katabole," here translated "evolution," is said to mean the descent of Solar Man into material conditions.

The formula, "He who has an ear, let him hear," is used by Apollonius as an appeal to the intuition. Here he states the broad principle: The man who craves sensuality by that desire condemns himself to remain in the bondage of reincarnation and subject to the iron law of retribution which prevails in the lower spheres of existence.

But the esoterist, knowing that nothing binds him to the physical form of life save the longings of his own nature, patiently endures all the ills of physical existence, in full assurance that thru the purifications of his moral character he will teach deliverance.

Ch. 13: 11, 12

I saw another (constellatory) Beast rising out of the earth. He had two horns like a lamb, and he talked like a dragon. He is wielding all the authority of the first Beast in his presence and is causing the earth and all its inhabitants to worship the first Beast whose death-blow has healed.

INTERPRETATION

This Pseudo-Lamb represents the dual sex-nature, the double-edged sword, the Good and the Evil, the Vishuddha chakra, the two riders of the dun horse, here in a different impersonation.

He is the image on the material plane of the Lamb, who in the opening of the seven seals played the parts of the rider of the white horse.

Thus the Lamb and the Pseudo-Lamb bear the same relation to each other as do Eros, the Divine Love, and Pathos (Cupid), the Carnal Love, not, however, as the base passion, but in its more refined forms as sentimental yearning, religious fervor of the irrational sort, and all the emotional impulses.

He talks like a dragon, from this source originate religious cant, sentimental ethics, and erotic utterances generally; and he has all the potentialities of the first Beast, the phrenic nature, for unutterable vileness.

As a constellation, he is the Head of Medusa, the mortal Gorgon, called by the Jews Rosch Hasatan

Owing to its proximity to Aries this constellation was sometimes pictured wearing the two horns of the Ram, the Apocalyptic Lamb.

Ch. 13: 13-18

He makes great omens so that he may even make fire come down out of the sky to the earth in the sight of men. He keeps deluding those who dwell on the earth, thru the omens which he was permitted to make in sight of the Beast, saying to those who dwell on the earth that they should make an image to the Beast who has the stroke of the sword and came to life.

It was permitted (him) to bestow breath on it, the image of the Beast, so that the image of the Beast should not only talk, but also cause all (men) who might not worship the image of the Beast to be slain. He causes all (men), the small and the great, the rich and the poor, alike, the freemen and the slaves, to be given a brand on their right hand or on their forehead and that no one should be able to buy or to sell unless he has the brand, the name of the Beast, or the number of his name.

Here is cleverness: let him who has the intuitive mind compute the number of the Beast; for it is the number of a man, and his number of 666.

INTERPRETATION

Magic powers were attributed to Medusa, and talismans were made under its stella influence. The word "omen" signifies also a "talisman" or symbol drawn under the influence of some particular constellation or planetary aspect.

Cedrenus states that Perseus (the slayer of the Gorgon) taught the Persians the magic of Medusa, by means of which fire came down out of the sky. But, apart from all exoteric notions of ceremonial magic, the Pseudo-Lamb, as a principle in man, does indeed draw down "fire" from the intellectual sky. For the force which it represents produces all the grosser forms of psychism and is the agent of the so-called "miracles" of exoteric religion, the prodigies produced by erotic fervor, blind credulity and disordered imagination. And it is likewise the foul force employed in phallic sorcery.

It is also the irrational instinct of religionism, the vague yearning for something to worship, a reflection or shadow of the true principle, which prompts men to project a subjective image of the lower, personal mind and to endow it with human attributes and then to claim to receive "revelations" from it as the church does and has done; and this--the image of the Beast, or unpsychical mind --is their anthropomorphic God: a fabulous monster the worship of which has ever prompted men to fanaticism and persecution and has inflicted untold misery and dread upon the masses, as well as physical torture and death in hideous forms upon the many martyrs who have refused to bend their knee to this Gorgonean phantom of the beast-mind of man.

Truly, where the worshippers of this image of the Beast predominate, he whose brow and hand are not branded by this superstition, who neither thinks nor acts in accordance with it, suffers ostracism if not virulent persecution.

"Here is cleverness" means "here is a puzzle." The number of the Beast, as already explained, is simply "he phren" (lower mind), the letters of which, as numerals, total 666; while the Pseudo-Lamb is "akrasia" (sensuality), 333.

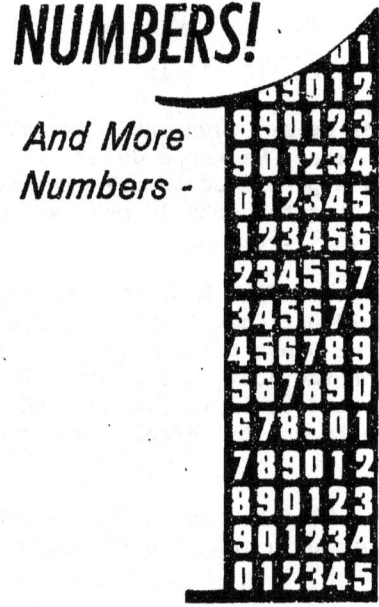

CHAPTER NO. 28

Ch. 14: 1-5

I saw; and, Behold! The Lamb standing on Mt. Sion and with him the 144,000 having their names and his father's name written on their foreheads.

I heard a voice from the sky, like the voice of many waters, like the voice of a great thunder; and the voice I heard was like (that) of lyrists playing on their lyres. They chanted a new lyric before the throne and before the four Beings and the elders, and no one could understand the lyric save the 144,000--they who had been bought from the earth.

These are the ones who were not defiled with women; for they are virgins. These are the ones who go along with the Lamb wherever he goes. These were bought from man--a firstling to the God and the Lamb. In their mouth was found no deceit; they are faultless.

INTERPRETATION

The Lamb is the fourth of the animal-symbols, or "beasts," and is identical with the Bowman on the white horse, the regent of the fourth somatic division. He is the Solar God, which is Iesous himself, the number of whose name is 888.

The Sun is the Lion when domiciled in Leo, which corresponds to the highest of the noetic chakras, and the Lamb when exalted in Aries, which corresponds to the numbers; and his being on Sion's hill also signifies that exaltation.

Here he is represented as being surrounded by his virginal powers, and a thunderous chorus preludes the next act in the drama, the conquest of the cardiac centers of the body. But this chorus, the fifth in the series, is only described, no words being given because, it is intimated, it would be unintelligible to the profane; and the conquest of the chakras of this division is given in less detail than are the others.

Ch. 14: 6, 7

I saw another Divinity flying in mid-sky, having an aeonian divine message to announce to those seated on the earth, to every people, tribe, tongue, and nation, and he said with a loud voice:

"Fear ye the God and to him give glory; for the hour of his judgment is come. Worship him who made the sky, the earth, the sea, and the springs of waters."

INTERPRETATION

This, the third of the conquests, is represented as a harvesting of the intellectual, psychic, and solarical principles, to which correspond respectively the cerebro-spinal column, the sympathetic nerve system, and the aureola. The action is therefore confined to the three higher centers corresponding to these principles; while the opening of the four lower chakras is given as a proclamation to each of the four lower principles seated in the somatic divisions.

An aeon is a definite life-period, as the life-time of a man, a generation, or the whole evolutionary period, the complete cycle of generation.

It is only the crude, unphilosophical notion that "eternity" is "a long period of time" that has caused the "authorized" translators of the New Testament to persist in giving aeons the meaning "eternal."

Time is not an entity, nor a thing per se, nor is eternity merely time indefinitely prolonged. Eternity is now, and Time is only a mental concept rising from the conscious change in the world called nature; whereas eternity is noumenal, changeless, extending neither into the past nor the future, but is an immeasurable present.

The aeonian evangel relates only to the cycle of generation--from which the Conqueror is about to be emancipated, after final judgment has been passed on his deeds during the aeon in which he as been successively incarnated among all the races and peoples who have had their lesser cycles in the vast period of human evolution.

Ch. 14: 8

Another, a second Divinity, came after (him), saying:

"She fell! Babylon the great fell--she who has made all the people drink of the wine of the lust of her prostitution."

INTERPRETATION

Babylon, elsewhere called the Woman in scarlet, personifies the physical nature, the carnal body, and the lust for existence inherent in its elements. It has "fallen" only in the sense that the consciousness of the Conqueror has become free from its trammels.

Babylon is the term used here because the Jews hated it so sorely on account of their long captivity there.

Ch. 14: 9-13

Another Divinity, the third, came after them, saying with a great voice:

"If any worships the Beast and his image and receives a brand on his forehead or on his (right hand), he also shall drink of the wine of the God's ardor which has been poured out raw into the wine-cup of his passion; and he shall be tormented with fire and sulphur in the presence of the holy Divinities and the Lamb.

"The smoke of their torment keeps going up throughout aeons of aeons, and no rest day or night are they having who worship the Beast and his image and whosoever receives the brand of his name. Here is the patience of the devotees, those who are keeping the commands of the God and the belief of Iesous."

I heard a voice from the sky saying:

"Write: Immortal are 'the dead' who die in the Master henceforth. 'Yea' says the Breath, 'that they may cease from their labors—but their words accompany them.'"

INTERPRETATION

The cosmic creative force becomes, in the spheres of generation, the force that engenders bodies and, in this respect, the worshippers of the Beast and his image, the personal God, partake of the power of generation and thereby are constantly undergoing the miseries of incarnation which they produce and in which they find no abiding peace.

But physical existence is in reality a purifactory discipline, like the fumigating with sulphur, a common practice with the ancients alluded to by Apollonius.

The followers of Iesous, the Solarical Mind, knowing this, endure life with patience and faith in cosmic processes.

The "dead" are the "living dead" who are "dead" while they live in darkness. They are the embodied Cosmic Force who "die in the Master" only when they attain liberation from the prison of their carnal body, ceasing then from their toil but retaining the fruition of their good works.

Ch. 14: 14-16

I saw; and Behold! a white cloud; and on the cloud (I saw) sitting (a Divinity) like the son of man, having on his head a golden crown and in his hand a sickle.

Another Divinity came out from the adytum, crying out with a loud cry to the (Divinity) seated on the cloud:

"Thrust out your sickle and reap, for to you has come the hour to reap—for the earth's harvest is dried up."

The (Divinity) seated on the cloud struck his sickle on the earth, and the earth was reaped.

INTERPRETATION

The fifth Divinity represents the First Logos here seated in the nimbus; for he is the overshadowing Self, the Uncrucified, or unincarnated. He reaps the scant harvest of the psychic nature.

Ch. 14: 17-20

Came from the adytum which is in the sky, another Divinity, he also having a keen sickle.

Another Divinity came out from the altar, he who has authority over fire; and he gave voice with a great shout to one who had the sickle, saying:

"Thrust out your sickle, and pick the grape clusters of the earth's vine; for her bunches of grapes are ripened."

The Divinity stuck his sickle into the earth and stripped the earth's vine and threw (the grapes) into the wine-vat, the great (womb) of the God's ardor. The wine-vat was trodden outside the city, and blood issues from the wine-vat up to the bridles of the horses, as far as 1600 stadia.

INTERPRETATION

The second of the two Reapers is the Second Logos, and he reaps the psychically dynamic nature, which on the plane of creative forces corresponds to the fivefold noetic group.

The "vine" of this conquest is identical with the "river Euphrates" of the three other conquests. It is the spinal cord, the path of the Five Pranas, or life-winds, which are now, by the exigencies of the fable, metamorphosed into bunches of grapes.

The solar forces, permeating and energizing the body's aura (wine-vat outside the city), produce a return current to the chakras of the four somatic divisions (bridles of the horses) and into the solar body, the 1600, or to "soma heliakon." It is a process analogous to the nutrition of the fetus in utero.

In stellar symbolism, each of these seven Divinities may be recognized among the constellations.

Thus, for instance, as Aries, the Sion of the fable, rises in the eastern horizon, the Eagle is near the zenith, together with the Swan and the Celestial Vulture, these being the three Divinities who are said to fly in mid-sky.

Figure 176.

CHAPTER NO. 29

Ch. 15: 1-4

I saw another constellation in the sky, great and wonderful, (and in it) seven Divinities having the seven scourges, the final (ordeals), for by them the God's ardor is finished.

I saw (a sheen), as it were a glassy sea, mixed with fire, and those who were Conquerors of the Beast, of his image, and of the number of his name, standing on the glassy sea, having lyres of the God. They keep chanting the lyric of Moses, a slave of the God, and the lyric of the Lamb, saying:

"Great and wonderful are thy works, O Master-God, the All-Dominator. Just and true are thy paths, thou Ruler of the Aeons. Who shall not fear, O Master, and glorify thy name? For thou art the Only Sanctified. For all the people shall come and worship before thee. For thy just deeds have been made manifest."

INTERPRETATION

This constellation is Taurus, the seven Divinities answer to the Pleiades, the group of stars situated in the neck of the stellar Bull, who is the symbol of solarical generative force.

In Old Testament mythology, Moses represented the Sun in Aries. His pean of victory after crossing the Red Sea (Ex. 14: 26-31; 15: 1-21) is probably the one referred to here. For the Red Sea symbolized the Sea of Generation. The crystalline and fiery sea is the celestial ether.

The Master-God, the All-Dominator, refers to Solar Man. The people who shall come and worship before thee are the cells of the body. This represents the improvement of the body that results from living the higher life on earth.

Ch. 15: 5-8; 16:1

After these (things) I saw; and, Behold! the adytum of the tent-temple of the evidence in the sky was opened. Came out from the adytum the seven Divinities having the seven scourges, clothed in flawless and brilliant stone and girded about their breasts with golden girdles.

One of the four Beasts gave the seven Divinities seven golden libation-saucers full of the ardor of the God who lives throughout the aeons of the aeons. And the adytum was filled with smoke from the glory of the God and from his inherent force, and no one was able to go into the adytum until the seven scourges of the seven Divinities should be finished. I heard a great voice from the adytum, saying to the Divinities:

"Go and pour out into the earth the seven libation-saucers of the God's ardor."

INTERPRETATION

The seven superlatively pure and dazzling Divinities who emerge from the adytum of the tabernacle are, like the Planetary Logos whose apparition is described in the opening vision, androgynous: each is a male figure with female breasts and wearing the girdle of Aphrodite.

Here the word "stethe" is used, which is applicable to either sex, while in the other instances the word is "mastoi," which applies more particularly to the female breasts.

The Hermaphroditos, or blended figure of Hermes (Mercury) and Aphrodite (Venus) was a familiar figure in Greek art.

In both the Greek and Jewish mystery-paraphernalia, the "ark" contained the male and female genitals, the body's creative organs.

As the Planetary Logos is inverted, mirrored upside down in the material world, these seven bisexual Divinities, while they have to do with the lowest of the body's divisions, are yet the highest and purest of all. For it is the purity of these centers that exalts man to the highest plane of existence. They are the finishers of the great work of regeneration and the precursors of the Conqueror on the white horse.

Each has a phialy, a shallow cup or saucer, used in pouring out drink-offerings to the Gods; and the libations they pour out consist of the primordial creative force-substance, the ether.

This ether, as symbolized by the glittering raiment of the seven Divinities, is colorless and without qualities of its own; but all qualities are imparted to it by the Thought of the God.

Paracelsus said: "All things are white when they come from the hand of God; he colors them afterward according to his pleasure."

These primordial elements are not "white," but are without color; and they are not later colored by an imaginary God but by cosmic processes of transformation.

CHAPTER NO. 30

Ch. 16:2

The first (Divinity) poured out his libation-saucer into the earth. There came to be a bad and painful sore on the men who had the brand of the Beast and who worshipped his image.

INTERPRETATION

The lowest division of the body, called "the earth," is the throne of the Pseudo-Seer; and the worshippers of the Beast and his image are the thought forms mirrored in this lowest reflector of the noetic consciousness, where they become distorted into the crude elemental notions of orthodox religion. These are symbolized as ulcerating; for the time has come for the complete eradication of the centers whence they radiate.

Ch. 16:3

The second Divinity poured out his libation-saucer into the sea. It became blood like a dead man's, and every psychic form of life in the sea died.

INTERPRETATION

The sea is the solar plexus center, the throne of the Dragon, the epithumetic, lower psychic nature. The libation eliminates from it the last vestiges of the passions and desires; and the aura of this division is suffused by the golden color of the pranas.

Ch. 16: 4-7

The third Divinity poured out his libation-saucer into the rivers and springs and the (waters) became blood. I heard the Divinity of the waters saying:

"Thou art just, O Master, who (forever) art, who wast, and who art sanctified; for thou didst pass this sentence upon (the followers of the Beast); for they poured out the blood of devotees and seers, and blood thou hast given them to drink; for they are deserving (of it)."

I heard (the Divinity hovering above) the altar saying:

"Verily, O Master-God, the All-Dominator, true and just are thy judgments."

INTERPRETATION

The rivers and springs are the throne of the Beast; it receives the golden color when the solar force reaches it. Its regent is the phrenic mind, the fourth chakra, which distorts and falsifies the intuitions reaching it from the noetic faculty.

The Divinity of the waters is the Zoon corresponding to this center, and the one hovering over the altar (Ch. 8:3) is the Zoon of the noetic center.

Here the word "coming," in the formula applied to the God is replaced by "sanctified"; for now the God has come, the future being merged in the present.

Ch. 16: 8, 9

The fourth Divinity poured out his libation-saucer upon the sun. (Authority) was given it to scorch men with fire. Men were scorched with great heat, and they profaned the name of the God who has authority over these scourges; but they did not reform to give him glory.

INTERPRETATION

The sun is the throne of the Sky-God, the Lion. The outpouring of the Serpentine Fire upon this center produces intense mental strain. The intellectual forces are represented as unrepentant and profane, simply because the Nous, undifferentiated Thought, is the "only sanctified."

Ch. 16: 10, 11

The fifth Divinity poured out his libation-saucer upon the throne of the Beast. His realm became darkened; and his (subjects) gnawed their tongues for pain and profaned the God of the sky because of their pains and sores; but they did not reform from their works.

INTERPRETATION

The Beast's throne, as a somatic division, is the heart region; but in a general way it includes the whole sympathetic nerve system of which the principle chakra, the solar plexus, is shared by the Dragon.

Ch. 16: 12

The sixth Divinity poured out his libation-saucer upon that great river, Euphrates. Its waters were dried up so that there might be prepared the path of the rulers who (come out) from the birthplace of the sun.

INTERPRETATION

In each of the four conquests, the sixth chakra is related to the cerebro-spinal axis and the five pranas, the solar or noetic forces, as the forces act on each of the four planes of existence to which the somatic divisions correspond.

In this final conquest, the waters of the Euphrates (nerve-force of the spinal system) are dried up; for henceforth the electric fires are to take their place permanently, as generation on the animalistic level has been conquered.

In the "sacred city" (solar body), the Euphrates becomes the main-street "of pure gold transparent as glass."

Ch. 16: 13-16

I saw (coming) out of the mouth of the Dragon, out of the mouth of the Beast, and out of the mouth of the Pseudo-Seer, three unpurified spirits, like frogs. For they are spirits of spectres, making omens; (and) they are going out among the rulers of the whole home-land to muster them for the battle of the great day (of the coming) of the God, the All-Dominator. (The God says:)

"Behold! I am coming (silently), like a thief. Immortal is he who stays awake and keeps on his outer garments so that he may not walk naked, and they see his shame."

They mustered them in the place which is called in Hebrew Harmagedon.

INTERPRETATION

We have again ascended six of the seven chakras of the spinal column. The three unpurified spirits are the three currents of the Serpentine Fire, and their force flows out to all adjacent parts at the sixth chakra, to muster them for the battle of the "great day," which means the activation of the Pineal gland, the Harmagedon.

The forces expelled by the drying up of the "Euphrates" issue from the three lower somatic centers and form a psychic entity analogous to the ghost of a deceased person: the after-death process of purification undergone by Solar Man occurs before death in him who "dies in the Master."

The Solar Body of disincarnated man, before entering upon its period of blissful rest in the higher world, must purge itself of all the evil forces and elements of the psychic nature; and these discarded elements remain in the lower world, the phantasmal realm, where they constitute, for a time, a psychic entity wearing the semblance of the departed personality, its ghost, shade, or specter --an elemental self, which is a congeries of all the impure and evil constituents thus rejected by Solar Man.

Ch. 16: 17-21

The seventh Divinity poured out his libation-saucer into the air. There came a great voice from the adytum of the sky, from the throne saying:

"He has been born!"

(Note: In the authorized version, it falsely reads, "It is done." (Rev. 17:17).

There came to be voices, lightnings, and thunders; and there came to be a great earthquake, such as has not happened since men were born upon the earth.

The great city came to be in three divisions. The cities of the people fell; and Babylon the great was remembered before the God to give to her the wine-cup of the wine of the ardor of his passion.

Every island fled, and the mountains were not found. Great hail keeps coming down from the sky upon men, and men profaned the God because of the scourge of the hail; for its scourge is exceedingly great.

INTERPRETATION

The fable here describes the great shock experienced by the activation of the Pineal gland; and "He has been born" means the birth of the Seer that results.

The voice from the adytum, that of the First Logos, announced the "birth from above" of the Conqueror, who thereupon appears on the white horse; but before this apparition is described, a digression is made to introduce explanatory matter.

The great city (physical body) is now three-divisional, the minor cities, the procreative centers, having been extirpated, sacrificed.

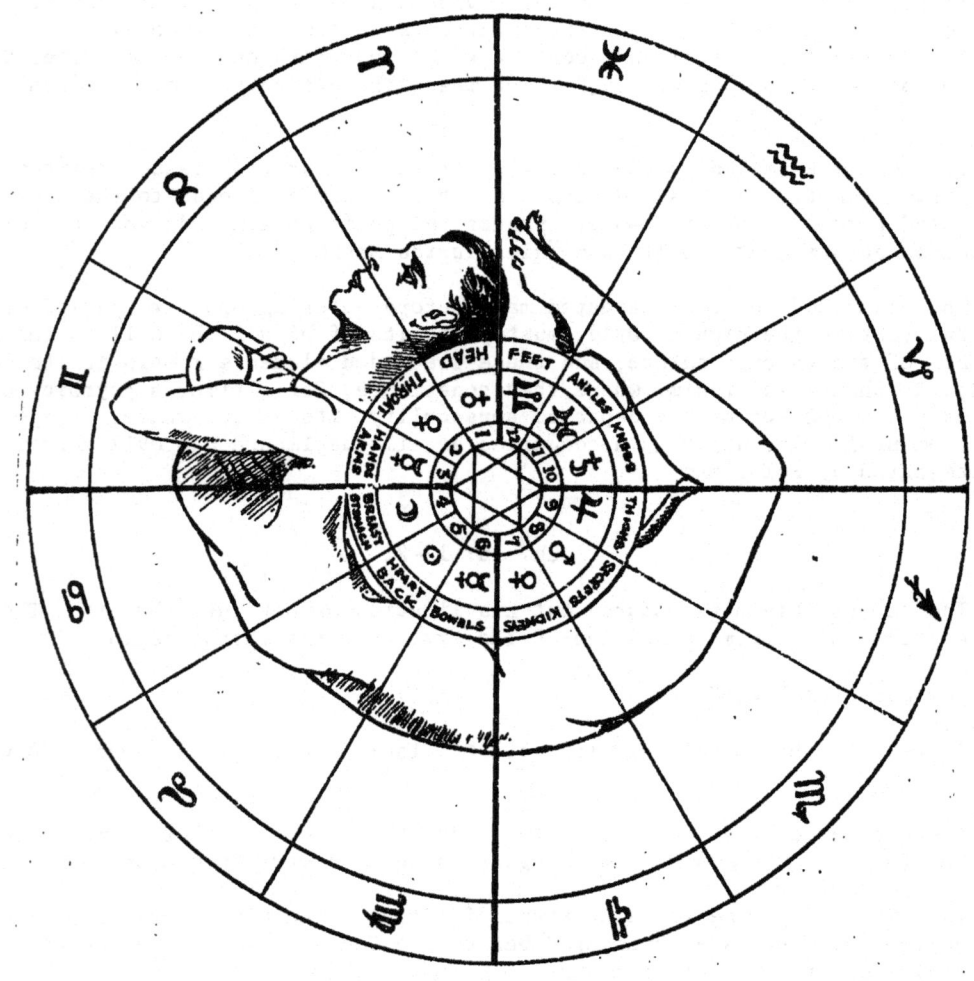

CHAPTER NO. 31

Ch. 17: 1-5

Came out of the seven Divinities who had the seven libation-saucers and talked with me, saying:

"Hither! I shall s ow you the judgment of the great prostitute who is sitting on the many water, with whom the rulers of the earth committed fornication, and those who dwell on the earth became intoxicated with the wine of her prostitution."

He carried me away in the Breath (-trance) into the desert; and I saw a Woman sitting on a scarlet Beast (having his mouth) full of names of profanity and having seven heads and ten horns. The Woman was arrayed in purple and scarlet, decked with gold, precious stones and pearls, having in her hand a golden wine-cup, full of the stenches and filth of her prostitution. On her forehead was a name written:

"A Mystery: Babylon the great, the 'Mother' of the (temple-) prostitutes and of the earth's stenches."

INTERPRETATION

The two Women of the Apocalypse are both Goddesses, in the ancient sense, precisely as the Angels are the lesser Gods of the ancient pantheon; and all these Gods and Goddesses are the personified powers and principles of the macrocosm and the microcosm.

Babylon symbolizes the human body; and, as the fallen Woman, she is a Goddess, the Magna Mater of the temple prostitutes in the Mystery-cult of Rhea, or Astarte.

Babylon, the human body, is most truly a Mystery to man and to science. The anatomists, physiologists, physicians, and psychologists who have studied this Mystery even on a strictly empirical and materialistic basis have gained more knowledge of the Divine Life manifested in the material world and have conferred vastly greater benefits on mankind than have all the exoteric religionists who have wasted their lives in formulating fantastic theologies and in coercing humanity into the worship of that figment of the unenlightened mind--the personal God.

But Babylon represents more than the physical body considered as a mere form composed of various tissues, a congeries of functional organs: It symbolizes also the broad principle of generation, of life confined to a physical form.

According to the arcane science, which Apollonius has presented in allegorical terms, forces are subtile elements; and the material elements are forces that have become inert.

All the forces and elements have their origin in the sun and are stored in the celestial ether, the Arche, or "first principle."

The Sun-clothed Virgin of the Sky, who gives birth to the male child, by the gestation of the solar body of the Conqueror, is the pure ether, the primordial force-substance.

In the spheres of animal-human generation, where that ether becomes differentiated into the gross material elements, she is the unchaste female, the mother of all that is abominable.

As an external form, a marvellous organism evolved by the Solar Body for its own purposes, the human body is the adytum of the God; but the elements composing it have become foul during the long ages of material evolution so that the Solar Body is ever being tainted and instigated to evil by the impure emanations and vicious impulses that have become inherent in the physical organism. It is thus a Mystery at once divine and infernal at which the Seer represents himself as gazing in wonder.

As a Goddess, the infernal Aphrodite, the depraved Virgo, symbolizes the anima bruta, or lower world-force, which is saturated with sexuality. In this role she holds a cup, which is the adjacent constellation Crater, the Mixing-bowl fabled to have belonged to Iacchos, the God of orgiastric revelry.

In this case, Babylon is used to symbolize the low, animalistic tendencies and propensities of the human body because Babylon was so terribly hated by the Jews on account of their long captivity there, and Apollonius (Pol) called himself a Jew (Acts. 21:39).

Ch. 17: 6-8

I saw the Woman intoxicated with the blood of the devotees and with the blood of the witnesses of Iesous. When I saw her, I gazed in wonderment, with great curiosity. Said the Divinity to me:

"Why did you wonder? I shall tell you the mystery of the Woman and of the Beast that was carrying her, which has the seven heads and ten horns. The Beast you saw was, and is not, and is about to come up out of the abyss and go to destruction. Those who dwell on the earth (the men) whose name has not been registered on the scroll of life since the evolution of the world--will wonder when they look at the Beast because he was, as is not, and shall be present.

INTERPRETATION

The Red Dragon, the epithumetic, passional nature, is the principle which, in close alliance with the Beast (phrenic mind) impels Solar Man to continue to incarnate; and the Dragon thus sustains the Woman, who typifies physical existence.

He rises from the abyss, the impure elements, and is again disintegrated in them when the Solar Body is purified.

The formula, "was, is not, and shall be present," merely expresses in an enigmatical way the Platonic doctrine that in the spheres of generation "nothing is, but all things are becoming"; that is, in the phenomenal world nothing partakes of permanency, but "all things are being created and disintegrated, coming into existence and passing into new forms."

Those who have not been registered on the scroll of life are simply the uninitiated.

Ch. 17: 9-11

"Here is the intuitive mind that has cleverness: the seven heads are seven mountains where the woman is sitting on them; and they are seven rulers (of whom) the five have fallen, and the one is, and the other has not yet come; and when he does come, he must abide a little while. The Beast which was and is not is himself also an eighth and is (an emanation) from the seven--and to destruction he is going.

INTERPRETATION

The seven heads of the Dragon are, like those of the Beast, the seven cardinal desires; but in the one they are mental and in the other instinctual; and the seven mountains are the Seven Chakras thru which they manifest during incarnation, the Woman being then seated on them, and they dominate in turn the seven incarnations thru which the neophyte must pass in conquering them. The irreclaimable residue of the epithumetic principle, which goes to form the after-death specter, or elemental self, is the eighth, "the son of perdition."

We observe that the Conqueror is represented in the drama as being in the sixth of the series of seven incarnations, so that five of them have perished and the seventh is yet to come. Hence, the Dragon, later on in the drama, is again imprisoned in the abyss and cannot be utterly slain until the seventh and last incarnation.

Ch. 17: 12-14

"The ten horns which you saw are ten rulers who have not yet received a realm; but they receive authority as rulers one hour with the Beast. They have our purpose; and their force and authority they pass along to the Beast. These will battle with the Lamb, and the Lamb will conquer them; for he is Master of masters and Ruler of rulers; and those who (go along) with him are called the chosen and reliable."

INTERPRETATION

The ten horns symbolize the five pranas, each of which is dual, positive and negative, on this plane, where they are merely the life-winds, or vital forces. They are not related to the chakras as the elements are, and hence are said to have no realm as yet; but later they have the spinal axis for their realm when the Lamb has conquered them.

Exuberant animal vitality, by intensifying the passional nature, tends away from the higher plane; hence these forces are represented as being inimical to Solar Man, yet they are to be conquered and utilized in a beneficial manner.

The forces subdued are here classified according to the three lower degrees of initiation in the early Christian secret society.

Ch. 17: 15-18

Also he says to me:

"The waters you saw, where the prostitute is sitting, are national mobs, peoples, and tongues.

"The ten horns you saw on the Beast--these shall abhor the prostitute and shall make her destitute and naked and shall devour her flesh and consume her with fire.

"For the God put it in their hearts to carry out his purpose, to carry (it) out (as their own) one purpose and to give their realm to the Beast until the instruction of the God should be finished.

"And the Woman you saw is the great city which has a realm (extending) over the rulers of the earth."

INTERPRETATION

The waters are the great sea of generated life, humanity in its vast cycle of physical and psychical evolution, which comprises all lesser racial and subracial cycles, in each of which every one plays one's part; and the whole mighty tide of life slowly works out the ultimate purpose.

Even the minor forces of man have in them the impulse of this purpose of the Solar God so that he who runs counter to it invites disorders and destruction from the very forces that normally vitalize and invigorate his physical form.

The "rulers of the earth" are the underlying forces of the physical world.

"Neither height nor depth can measure the possibilities of the human soul."

CHAPTER NO. 32

Ch. 18: 1-3

After these (instructions) I saw another Divinity coming down out of the sky, having great authority; and the earth was lit up by his glory. He cried out with a strong voice, saying:

"She fell! The great Babylon fell and became a haunt of ghosts, a prison of every filthy specter, and a cage of every filthy and loathsome bird (of prey). For by the wine of the lust of her prostitution all the people have fallen. The rulers of the earth committed fornication with her; and the merchants of the earth by the force of her lewdness grew rich."

INTERPRETATION

The Apocalyptic hero, having conquered in the ordeals of his initiation, achieving the solarical rebirth, has risen above the illusions of earthly life and taken his place among the eternal Gods.

The exhortations and lamentations that follow the declaration of the radiant Divinity concerning the fall of Babylon are of a general nature, applying to the aggregate of humanity and not at all to the Conqueror. For, as there are two crucifixions, so there are two falls, one from the sun and one from the moon.

The fall of Babylon (human body) is the fall into mortal corruption, the desecretation by man of his own body, which he has converted into holds of iniquity.

But, as to the Conqueror, the fall of Babylon is the reverse of this; for it means the conquest, subjugation, and purification of the body.

The people, rulers, and merchants who were debauched by the great prostitute are the three lower castes, the toiling, combative, and commercial classes, while the Divinities symbolize the fourth and highest class, the enlightened.

Ch. 18: 4-24

I heard another voice from the sky saying:

"Come out from her, O my people, so that you may not have partnership in her sins and so that you may not receive her scourges. For her sins have followed (you) up to the sky, and the God has held in memory her deeds. Pay her back as she also paid back, and double to her twofold, according to her works.

"In the wine-cup which she poured out, pour out for her a double (draught). As much as she glorified herself and grew lewd, so much give her of torment and mourning; for in her heart she keeps saying:

"I sit enthroned a queen and am not a widow; and I shall not put on mourning.'

"Therefore in one day shall come her scourges--death, mourning, and hunger--and she shall be consumed by fire. For strong is the Master God who judged her.

-71-

"The rulers of the earth who committed fornication and were lustful with her shall weep and wail over her when they look at the smoke of her conflagration, standing afar thru fear of her torment, saying:

"Woe! Woe! The great city, the strong city, Babylon. For in one hour has come your judgment.'

"The merchants of the earth shed tears and mourn over her, for no one buys their stock any more--the stock of gold, silver, precious stones, pearls, byssus, purple, and silken (fabrics); and all citrus wood, every ivory utensil, every utensil of very precious wood, of bronze, or iron and of marble; and cinnamon, amomum, incense, ointment, frankincense, wine, oil, flour, wheat, cattle and sheep; and of horses and chariots--and all bodies and souls of men!"

"The fruits your soul lusted for are gone, and all dainty and radiant (charms) have perished from you; and (your lovers) shall never more find them (in you).

"The merchants of these wares who were encircled by her shall stand afar thru fear of her torment, shedding tears and mourning, saying:

"Woe! Woe! The great city--she who was arrayed in byssus (fabric), purple, and scarlet, and covered with gold, precious stones, and pearls! For in one hour all this wealth has come to destitution.'

"And every sailing-matter and every crew on the ships, sailors, and as many as toil on the sea, stood afar and cried out, on seeing the smoke of her conflagration, saying:

"What city is the equal of the great city?'

"And they threw dust on their heads and cried out, weeping and sorrowing, saying:

"Woe! Woe! The great city, by whom all were enriched who have ships on the sea from her bountifulness! For in one hour she has come to destitution.'

"Rejoice over her, O sky, and ye devotees, apostles, and seers! For the God has passed sentence upon her in accordance with your decision."

A lone Divinity, the strong one, took up a stone, like a great millstone, and threw it into the sea, saying:

"Thus with a rush shall Babylon, the great city, be thrown down and shall not be found anymore.

"The voice of lyrists, musicians, fluitists, and trumpeters shall not be heard in thee any more; no craftsman, of whatever craft, shall be found any more in thee; the voice of a millstone shall not be heard in thee any more; the light of a lamp shall not shine in thee any more; and the voice of the bridegroom and of the bride shall not be heard in thee anymore. For thy merchants were the magnates of the earth. For by thy witchcraft all the people were deluded."

In her was found the blood of seers and devotees and of all who have been sacrificed on the earth.

INTERPRETATION

The four castes take part in the rejoicing and lamentation over the prospective fall of Babylon, an event which, for the multitude, lies in the extremely remote future.

The highest caste is given as threefold, composed of devotees, apostles, and seers. But they utter no rejoicing, the Divinities acting as their spokesman.

The profane, comprising the rulers or dominant warlike class, the merchants or trading class, and the sailors, the toiling masses of the sea of life, indulge in lamentations over the fall of the great city.

For the present and for ages to come, in all lands alike, Astarte remains enthroned on the red Dragon; and in this century her cup is more overflowing with abominations, and the traffic in the bodies of men and women goes on more briskly than in the days when Apollonius made his copy of the Hindu Scroll.

The destruction of the Apocalyptic Babylon (animalistic tendencies and propensities in the human body) will come only when humanity shall have learned to loathe the lusts of the flesh and to love the glories of angelic life.

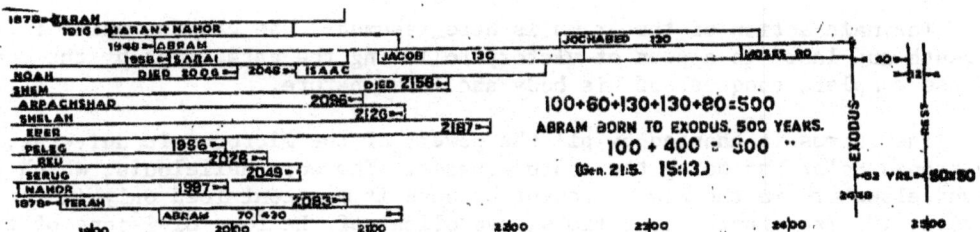

We received the above chart from one of our customers, George H. Gabus, New York. He has purchased many, many copies of our facsimile of THE BOOK OF JASHER.

CHAPTER NO. 33

Ch. 19: 1-8

After these (lamentations) I heard (a chorus), as it were the voice of a vast throng in the sky, saying:

"Hallelouia! The deliverance, glory, and force are our God's. For true and just are his judgments: for he has judged the great prostitute (his own body) who corrupted the earth with her prostitution, and he has avenged the blood of his slaves (Ida, Pingala, and Sushumna nadis) at her hand."

And once more they have said:

"Hallelouia! Her smoke keeps going up throughout the aeons of the aeons!"

The 24 elders and the four Beings fell down and worshipped the God seated on the throne, saying:

"Amen. Hallelouia!"

A voice came out of the throne saying:

"Praise ye our God (Solar Man), all ye his slaves (organs of the body) and ye who fear him (carnal thoughts), both the small and the great."

And I heard (a chorus), as it were the voice of a vast throng, as the voice of many waters, and as the voice of mighty thunders, saying:

"Hallelouia! For the Master God, the All-Dominator, has become ruler.

"Let us rejoice and become ecstatic, and let us give to him the glory; for the marriage of the Lamb (Pineal gland) has come, and his wife (Pituitary gland) has made herself ready. To her was given (the right) to clothe herself in byssus (-vesture) brilliant and pure; for these are the awards to the devotees."

INTERPRETATION

The main action of the drama is here resumed: the chorus, which is the seventh and last, is a pean of victory following the attainment by the Conqueror of the complete conquest of his body and lower nature.

The chorus is chanted by all the powers of the microcosmic universe, the enthroned Solar Man being the chorus-leader. The word Hallelouia, which is not found elsewhere in the New Testament because it was contained only in the Hindu scroll, is here chanted four times, symbolical of the four divisions of the body.

The marriage was one of the symbolic rites in the Greek Mysteries; and universally in mysticism Solar Force is represented as the male and physical matter as the female.

Byssus was a fine cloth, naturally of a yellow color, affected by oriental devotees. It represents the auric color of a saintly man.

Ch. 19: 9, 10

And to me (the Divinity) says:

"Write: Immortal are they who are invited to the wedding dinner of the Lamb."

And (again) he says to me:

"These arcane doctrines are the God's."

I fell down before his feet to worship him; but he says to me:

"See to it (that you do) not. I am a fellow-slave with you and with your brothers who have the evidence of Iesous. Worship the God."

(For "the evidence of Iesous" is the Power of Seership.")

INTERPRETATION

Absolute certainty of the Immortal Nature, the conscious Real Self, can be had only thru the sacred trance in which all the lower faculties are placed in abeyance, the clamor of the senses, emotions, and thoughts completely stilled so that in the perfect peace and silence of the Mind the voice of the Real Man may become audible.

This trance-state can be attained only thru the action of the Serpentine Fire, the dynamic working-force of the Solar Body, the Cosmic Creative Force.

Ch. 19: 11-16

I saw the sky opened; and, Behold! a white horse (appeared), and he who was riding him is called Believable and True (Solar Man), and with justice he judges and gives battle (to the lower forces of the body).

His eyes are like a blaze of fire, and on his head are many diadems; and (on his forehead) he has a name written which no one knows save himself. He is clothed in a garment dyed with blood; and his name is called "The Logos of the God."

The armies in the sky were following him on the white horse wearing byssus (-robes), white and pure.

From his mouth keeps flashing forth a keen sword, that with it he might chastise the people. He shall rule them with an iron wand. He is treading the wine-vat (overflowing with) the wine of the ardor of the passion of the God. He has on his garment and on his thigh the name written, "Ruler of rulers and Master of masters."

INTERPRETATION

The hero on the white horse is the Second Logos, the incarnating Ego. He is now the Conqueror who by indomitable will has completed the telestic work and is no longer the inverted Logos. For here he wears the aspect of Mars, the War God, who, in the older mythology, is the God of Generation. He rules with a rod of iron, the metal of Mars. He treads the wine-vat of generative force, and he has his title written on his thigh (an euphemism for phallos) (as in Old Testament usage--Gen. 24:2).

This means that the Conqueror has mastered all the lower forces of his body and attained the state of sinless purity, having eradicated from his nature everything related to the lower phases of physical existence.

He now goes forth to the final battle with the elemental self, the Tartarean ghost of his now defunct psycho-material personality.

Ch. 19: 17, 18

I saw a lone Divinity standing in the sun. He cried out with a great voice saying to all the birds (of prey) that fly in mid-sky (evil thoughts in the brain):

"Come! Flock together to the dinner of the great God so that you may devour the flesh of the rulers, the commanders, the strong warriors, the flesh of horses and of their riders, and the flesh of all, free and slave, both small and great."

INTERPRETATION

The "lone" Divinities are the Chief Divinities, corresponding to the Zoa; here the one standing in the Sun is Mikael, he who drove the Dragon from the sky.

The elemental self is the essence of impurity in the psychic and material elements; and as a sort of by-product, so to say, of the evolutionary aeons, it is a concretion of all that was evil in each incarnation during the aeonian sojourn of the Ego in the spheres of generation: It is therefore the carnal element, of kings, warriors, and of all the other personalities assumed by the incarnating Self in the drama enacted by humanity.

Ch. 19: 19-21

I saw the beast and the rulers of the earth and their armies drawn together to do battle with the Rider on the White Horse and his army. The Beast was captured and with him the Pseudo-Seer who made the omens in his sight, by which he deluded those who had received the brand of the Beast and the worshippers of his image.

The two (beasts) were cast alive into the lake of fire which flames with sulphur; and the rest were slain by the sword of the Rider on the White Horse, which kept flashing forth from his mouth; and all the birds (of prey) were filled with their flesh.

INTERPRETATION

In this fabulous battle, the instinctual and phrenic principles of the elemental congeries are apprehended and thrown into the astral fire of the phantasmal world, where disintegration is their final fate.

CHAPTER NO. 34

Ch. 20: 1-3

I saw a Divinity come down from the sky having the key of the abyss and a chain in his hand. He apprehended the Dragon, the archaic Snake who is the Accuser and the Adversary, and bound him for a thousand years and cast him into the abyss and locked and sealed (it) atop of him so that he should not delude the people anymore until the thousand years should be finished; and after that he must be loosed a short time.

INTERPRETATION

Since the hero of the Apocalypse is represented as being in the sixth incarnation of the seven composing the cycle of initiation, he has one more earth-life to go thru and cannot yet completely destroy the epithumetic principle. Instead it is placed in durance for a thousand years, after which it must be freed when the hero reincarnates; and then it will be speedily exterminated forever.

This seventh incarnation is the last of the Seven Rulers who are the Seven Heads of the Dragon; and of this Ruler it is said that "when he does come, he must abide a short time."

In placing the time between incarnations at a thousand years, Apollonius follows Plato who gives that period.

Ch. 20: 4-6

I saw thrones and those seated on them; and judgment was passed on them. And (I saw) the souls of those who had been beheaded on account of the evidence of Iesous and on account of the arcane doctrine of the God; also those who did not worship the Beast or his image and did not receive his brand on their forehead and on their hand; and they came to life and ruled with the Anointed for a thousand years; (but) the rest of the dead did not come to life again until the thousand years were finished. This is the first resurrection.

Immortal and holy is he who has part in the first resurrection; on such the second death does not hold sway, but they shall be sacrificers to the God and his Anointed; and they shall rule with him for the thousand years.

INTERPRETATION

When the Beast and the Pseudo-Seer were cast into the astral fire and the Dragon was incarcerated in the abyss, they made their final exit from the stage. The Conqueror has annihilated the bogus Lion and the bogus Lamb; but in the next incarnation, he will have to fight and destroy the Dragon, the bogus Arche-Logos.

The Apocalyptic drama covers but the one incarnation; and so, rather than leave in uncertainty the issue of the final combat between the Conqueror and the

Dragon, Apollonius here introduces a side-scene in which he first explains in general what happens to Solar Man during the periods between incarnations and then, carrying into the future the story of the Conqueror, describes the final battle in the next incarnation, resulting in the final defeat and destruction of the Dragon.

The thrones and those enthroned on the thrones represent a typical individual in a series of incarnations, after each of which, upon the demise of the physical body, the enthroned Solar Man passes judgment upon the deeds and misdeeds on the planes of thought, sensation, emotion, and action, of the lower self during the preceding earth-life.

All the pure and noble thoughts, sentiments, aspirations, and memories are retained and remain in the Eternal Mind, the Nous, throughout the season of subjective peace and bliss which Solar Man then experiences. But all the worthless and evil elements are rejected and left to remain dormant in the lower psychic world, dying the "second death," and coming to life only when Solar Man again descends into the spheres of generation.

Thus man's own past is his personal "Devil," the ancient serpent trailing thru the ages and accusing him day and night before his Inner Being, who is his righteous Judge.

Ch. 20: 7-10

When the thousand years are ended, the Adversary shall be turned loose from his prison and come out to delude the people who are in the four corners of the earth (the Gog and Magog), to bring them together for battle, the number of whom is as the sand of the sea.

They went up on the width of the earth and surrounded the fortress of the devotees and the beloved city. And fire came down out of the sky and consumed them. The Accuser, the deluder of them, was thrown into the lake of fire and sulphur, where also are the Beast and Pseudo-Seer; and they shall be tormented day and night throughout the aeons of the aeons.

INTERPRETATION

Here is foretold the fate of the Dragon, the epithumetic principle, whose host of desires, passions, and longings is indeed as the sand of the sea. But they now have no lodging-place in the purified nature of the Conqueror and exist only as surviving impressions and impulses impressed like phonographic records on the plastic World Soul, and as a malignant composite spectral entity they assail him from without.

The purifying fire of the Kundalini Force obliterates these collective phantoms; and their focal center, the Dragon in his capacity as the "eighth," shares the doom of the bogus Lion and the bogus Lamb.

The words "Gog" and "Magog" mean "Gog, kind of the land of Magog."

It is a true parallel from the Jewish mythology and indicates that whoever interpolated those words understood to some extent the esoteric meaning of the Apocalypse and also the inner sense of the Old Testament fables.

In fact, no real esotericist could possibly fail to perceive the general meaning of the Apocalyptic allegory; and the solution of its peculiar puzzles calls only for the exercise of ingenuity on the part of any one who understands the arcane science.

But down thru the ages the esotericists have smiled and remained silent while the exoteric "Church Fathers" and their successors have tortured this magnificent epic into a theological nightmare, trying to weave it around their personal God, his Son Jesus and the mythical heaven.

For if the "orthodox" had discovered its secret nature, the Apocalypse would have shared the fate of the learned "Porphyry's treatise on Christianity," which was burned by decree of the Roman Emperor.

Ch. 20: 11-15

I saw a great white throne and (the God) seated on it, from whose face there fled the earth and the sky; and a place was not found for them.

I saw the dead, the great, and the small standing before the throne; and (their) scrolls were unrolled. Another scroll was unrolled, which is (the Lamb's scroll) of life. The dead were judged from the (records) written in (their) scrolls, according to their works.

Death and the Unseen were thrown into the lake of fire. This is the second death--the lake of fire.

If any one was not found registered in the (Lamb's) scroll of life, he was thrown into the lake of fire.

INTERPRETATION

Here the action of the drama is again resumed. The initiate has severed himself from the lower life; and by thus renouncing everything pertaining to the physical form of existence, he is morally and dynamically in the same condition as is the disincarnated man so that his past must be adjudicated in the same way. But, whereas the after-death judgment of the uninitiated Solar Body involves only its last preceding earth-life, the Conqueror must render an account of all his antecedent incarnations: the records in their scrolls are reviewed, and then all are summed up in the Lamb's great scroll of life, the comprehensive record of the incarnating Self.

All his deeds in the great sea of sensuous life, all the things he ever did in the physical and psychic worlds, spring to life in the Eternal Memory and are all passed upon by the inexorable Judge; and whatever element in the aeon-evolved character of man that is found unworthy of Life Eternal is hurled into the symbolical fire of the chaos, there to disintegrate in the second death.

In this there is no shadow of that exoteric and silly notion, the "vicarious atonement."

According to the philosophy of Apollonius, Seer and Initiate, the great Teacher of the first century, rigid justice rules all worlds of existence.

CHAPTER NO. 35

Ch. 21: 1-5

I saw a new sky and a new earth--for the first sky and the first earth have passed away, and the sea is no more.

I saw the great city, New Hierousalem, coming down out of the sky, from the God, made ready as a bride bedecked for her husband. I heard a great voice from the throne, saying:

"Behold! the tent of the God is with man, and he shall pitch tent with them. They shall be his people and the God himself shall be with them, their God! He shall wipe away every tear from their eyes; and there shall be no more death, nor shall there be mourning, lamentation, or pain anymore. For the material elements have passed away."

Said the (Master) seated on the throne: "Behold! I am making a new universe."

And to me he says: "Write: These arcane doctrines are believable and true."

INTERPRETATION

In the prelude to the first act of the drama (4:11) the Powers chant a pean to the God who brought into existence the universe. But now that microcosmic "universe," the lower self which had been evolved during the generative aeons, has fulfilled its purpose and is superseded by a new Universe, a new cycle of solarical evolution transcendent in glory.

Ch. 21: 6-8

And (again) he said to me:

"He has been born, (but) I am the Alpha and the O, the Origin and the Perfection. To him who thirsts, I shall give of the spring of the water of life as a free gift. The Conqueror shall obtained the universe, and I will be a God to him; and he shall be a son to me.

"But, for the cowardly, the unbelieving, the malodorous, murderers, fornicators, sorcerers, worshippers of phantoms, and all liars, their part (shall be) in the (symbolical) lake which flames with fire and sulphur--which is the second death."

INTERPRETATION

The Hindus held that the First Logos, the enthroned God, who is the source of life and its ultimate goal, is never incarnated. Then the First Logos could be nothing else but the Solar Orb itself, for it is really the source of all life upon the earth.

The Second Logos is the incarnating Self, a Spark of the Sun; and man on earth is the Third Logos, who becomes the Son of Perfection as he conquers his own body and thus achieves what is termed the Second Birth.

Yet these three are in reality one, the Divine Man manifested on three planes of life.

The Hindus taught that if carnal man becomes irredeemably wicked, his fate is the second death, the reverse of the second birth: his psychic self decomposes in the fiery subtle elements even as the physical body is resolved into its original elements when abandoned by the animating principle. The second death means the obliteration of the individual consciousness. This entire theory is open to question.

The second birth leads to the attuning of the individual consciousness with the universal, which state is termed Cosmic Consciousness.

Ch. 21: 9-14 (Interpretation Included)

Come one of the seven Divinities who had the seven libation-saucers who were charged with the seven last scourges, and he talked with me, saying:

"Hither! I shall show you the bride--the Lamb's wife."

In this symbolism, the Pineal gland (male) represents the Lamb, and the wife is the Pituitary gland (female).

"He carried me away in the Breath (-trance) to a mountain great and high."

The mountain represents the Skull. Man's brain is the greatest, highest, and most mysterious of all structures. In his brain Man is the God of the whole earth. In his brain he rises to the sun, the sky, to infinity, to eternity. The power of man's brain is the greatest of all cosmic structures.

When the Lamb (Pineal) receives the energizing and inspirational force of the Solar Fire, passed on by the wife (Pituitary), there comes speedily to man the Cosmic Sight of the Seer. When this occurred in the initiation of the neophyte in the Ancient Mysteries, he almost involuntarily cried out with great joy: "O Pure Light! Hail New Born Light! I am initiated and become holy!" --Pike.

"And (he) showed me the holy city Hierousalem (deathless Solar Body), coming down out of the sky from the God (Sun), having the God's (Sun's) glory-- (and this), her luminary (solar fire of the Pituitary), was like a precious stone, like an opal crystal glittering."

This is the arc of electric light from the Pituitary which emits a faint roseate hue, an opalescent, bluish glitter.

"Having a wall great and high." The aura.

"Having 12 gateways." The 12 orifices of the body.

"And at the gateways 12 Divinities (the 12 gods of the Zodiac, representing the 12 cosmic forces). And (on the gateways) names inscribed, which are (the names) of the 12 tribes of the children of Is-Rae-El (12 zodiacal signs)."

"On the east were three gateways, on the north three gateways, on the south three gateways, and on the west three gateways."

The tribes (zodiacal signs) are in four triads, assigned to the four regions of the earth or space, and representing the four seasons of the year.

"The wall of the city had 12 foundations, and on them (were inscribed) the 12 names of the 12 apostles of the Lamb."

The aura of the body (wall of the city) has 12 force centers, where the 12 cosmic forces are focussed on the microcosm. These focal centers are dynamically related to the 12 orifices of the body--the 12 gateways of the city, also corresponding to the 12 zodiacal signs, the 12 apostles of the Lamb, the Lamb in this case representing the Sun making 13.

The Zodiac was the Master's Wheel of Life. In its symbology is contained the ancient secret of man's origin and destiny.

The wall of the city (aura) has 12 foundations, the 12 cosmic forces. In ancient symbology the foundation of all things is Spirit (Solar), upon which rests the structures of whatever is manifested.

Biblical critics hold that Ez=Ra (Az-Ra or Zer-Oa) compiled from ancient literature the first five books of the Bible, commonly but erroneously called the Books of Moses. That it was he who invented the name Israel, in which he combined El, the god of the Jews, with Isis and Ra, the Nature Goddess and the Sun God of the Egyptians, making it Is-Ra-El.

Ch. 21: 15-21

The (Divinity) who was talking with me had for a measure a golden reed to measure the city, its gateways, and its wall. The city lies four-square, and its length is as great as its width. He measured the city with the reed, by statia, 12,000; its length, width, and heighth are equal. And he measured its wall, 144 cubits (including) the measure of a man, that is, of a Divinity. The building-material of its wall as opal; and the city was pure gold, like clear glass.

The foundations of the wall of the city were ornamented with every precious stone: the first foundation was opal; the second, sapphire; the third, chalcedony; the fourth, aqua-marine; the fifth, sardonyx; the sixth, carnelian; the seventh, chrysolite; the eighth, beryl; the ninth, topaz; the tenth, chrysoprase; the eleventh, jacinth; and the twelfth, amethyst. The 12 gateways were 12 pearls, and each one of the 12 gateways was (carved) from a single pearl.

INTERPRETATION

We have explained that the cubical city, when unfolded, becomes a cross, symbolizing the human form, with feet together and arms extended at right angles. It is the Solar Body, to some heliakon, the numerical value of the Greek words being 1600; the number of Jewish miles in 12000 stadia.

The aura, he doxa, gives the number 143, to which is added an alpha, 1, that being the vowel and number of primeval man, or Divinity.

The aura is a brilliant opalescence, self-luminous, and the solar body has the appearance of transparent gold.

The 12 precious stones are not all identified with certainty, as some of the Greek names are dubious. Placed in a circle, as if incorporated in the aura, these colored stones form approximately the prismatic scale and are thus identical with the rainbow which encircles the throne of the God, mentioned in Rev. 4:3.

Ch. 21: 21-27

The main street of the city was pure gold, transparent as glass. No adytum did I see in it; for the Master God, the All Dominator, and the Lamb are its adytum.

The city has no need of the sun, nor of the moon, to shine in it; for the God's glory lights it; and its lamp is the Lamb, and the people (who are of the delivered) shall walk in its light; and the rulers of the earth keep bringing their glory into it. Its gateways shall not be closed by day--for there shall be no night there. They shall bring the glory and the honor of the people into it; and there shall not enter into it anything profane, nor he who created a stench and (acts) a lie, but only those who are registered in the Lamb's scroll of life.

INTERPRETATION

The main street represents the spinal cord. But the complex structure of the gross body, with its organs, glands, and functions, is not duplicated in the solar body, formed of etheric fire, and is in direct relation with, and sustained by, the cosmic forces. And so "no adytum did I see in it."

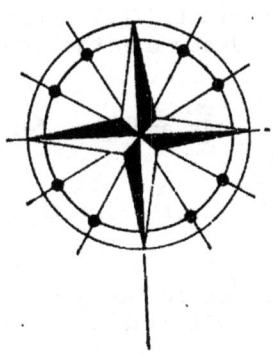

Time is like a river made up of the events which happen, and its current is strong; No sooner does anything appear than it is swept away, and another comes in its place, And will be swept away too.
Marcus Aurelius Antoninus

CHAPTER NO. 36

No. 22: 1-5

He showed me a pure river of the water of life, clear as crystal, flowing out of the throne of the God and of the Lamb, in the middle of its main street; and on one side of the river and on the other was the tree of life, producing twelve fruits according to the months, each one yielding its fruit; and the leaves of the tree were for the healing of the people--and the accursed (function of animalistic generation) shall not exist anymore (in the angelic world).

The throne of the God and of the Lamb shall be in it, and his slaves will serve him; they will see his face, and his name (will be) on their foreheads. There will be no night there; and they will have no need of lamp or light of the sun; for the Master God will give them light, and they will rule throughout the aeons of the aeons.

INTERPRETATION

The river of water of life is the spinal fluid, flowing from the brain (throne of God and of the Lamb).

The two trees of life on each side of the river are the Ida and Pingala nadis.

The twelve fruits produced, according to the months, represent the psycho-physical Seed born in the Solar Plexus every $29\frac{1}{2}$ days in the life of man and woman after puberty, when the Moon is in the sign the Sun was in at the time of one's birth.

In the Bible this area of the body is termed the "House of Bread" because the Solar Plexus lies behind the stomach.

The church fathers had their Jesus born in Bethlehem (Mat. 2:1). The word Bethlehem is from Beth, house, and Lechem, bread; and so Jesus was the "Bread of Life" that came down from heaven (head) (Jn. 6:35, 41).

The leaves of the trees represent the nerves of the body and were for the healing of the people--the billions of cells of the body.

The "accursed" function of animalistic generation does not exist in the Solar Body.

This function produces a patho-physiological irritation in the parts involved caused by the friction of fornication, which the Bible calls "the motions of sin." (Rom. 7:5).

That "pleasurable" irritation provokes, for its relief, an expenditure of vital fluid in the process termed "orgasm," which ends the act and the pleasurable misery of the organs involved.

Most of the doctors don't know that this results in a vital damage to the male in particular, which nothing can repair, a vital loss which nothing can replace.

The throne of the God and of the Lamb are in the Solar Body; and his slaves (organs of the body) will serve him because he has mastered his body and made its organs serve him, instead of his being the slave of desire and lust, as the average man is.

There is no night nor darkness for the Solar Body and no need for either lamp or light.

Ch. 22: 6-9

He said to me:

"These arcane doctrines are believable and true. The Master God of the 'Breaths' of the Seers sent his Divinity to make known to his slaves the (perfections) which must be attained speedily. Behold! I am coming speedily. Immortal is he who observes the arcane doctrines of the teaching of this (Hindu) scroll."

"I (physical man-Ioannes-Apollonius) am he who was seeing and hearing these (things); and when I heard and saw, I fell down to worship before the feet of the Divinity who was making known these (things) to me. And he says to me:

"'See to it (that you do) not. I am a fellow-slave with you and with your brothers, the Seers, and those who observe the arcane doctrines of the teachings of this scroll. Worship the God!"

INTERPRETATION

The Breaths of the Seers are the differentiated forces of the Great Breath, used by the Seers in the telestic work. The Arch-Divinity of these creative forces is the Nous.

Nothing should be worshipped that has form or is individuated. The Cosmic Power alone is to be worshipped.

The Conquer obtains the universe not by being absorbed and obliterated by it, but by transcending the limitations of his own individual consciousness and partaking of Cosmic Consciousness.

As an individual, he loses nothing but his *imperfections*, and he gains the All, the *"Origin of the Perfection,"* making him the *Son of Perfection*.

And this state is Seership, which is not "prophecy," "second sight," nor sense-perception on any plane of consciousness, but is Direct Cognition of Reality.

Ch. 22: 10-16

And (again) he says to me:

"Do not seal up the arcane doctrines of the teachings of this scroll; for the season is near.

"The unjust, let him do injustice yet more; the sordid, let him be made yet more sordid; the just, let him do justice yet more; and the devotee, let him be made yet more devoted.

"Behold! I am coming speedily; and my wages are with me, to pay off each (laborer) as his work is.

"I am the Alpha and the O, the First (Adam) and the Last (Adam), the Origin and the Perfection.

"Immortal are those who are washing their robes so that they may have authority over the Tree of Life and may enter by the gateways of the city.

"Outside are the dogs, the sorcerers, the fornicators, the murderers, the phantom-servers, and every one who keeps sanctioning and acting a lie.

"I, Iesous (Solar Man), have sent my Divinity to give evidence to you of these (works depending) upon the Seven Societies. I am the Root and the offspring of David, his bright and Morning Star."

INTERPRETATION

The injunction not to seal up the teachings has been observed by the Apocalyptist; for while his scroll is written in veiled language, it is not "sealed" as in the case of a strictly occult book, which is written either in cipher or secret code and cannot be read without a key.

Mystical works intended for general circulation are usually worded obscurely, being designed to elicit and cultivate the intuitive faculty of the reader; and they are almost without exception, disconnected, fragmentary, and often interspersed with irrelevant passages.

But the Apocalypse contains its own key and is complete in itself, coherent and scrupulously accurate in detail. The puzzles it contain are not intended to mislead or confuse; on the contrary, they serve to verify the correct interpretation of the fable.

The book is not sealed to any one who has the developed intuitive faculty and for whom the season, the springtime of noetic unfoldment, is near.

While the growth of the inner nature is a slow process during many incarnations, the recognition of the actuality of Solar Man, of the immanent higher Mind, comes upon man suddenly. As Apollonius reiterates, the Logos comes speedily, unexpectedly, as a thief in the night; and when it does come, there is a balancing of merits and demerits.

If his body and mind are sufficiently purified, the mystic tree of Life (Solar Fire) is his and by means of it he enters the Holy City. Otherwise he remains with "those without," the exotericists, until he shall have "washed his robes" and thereby gained the right to employ the "Breaths of the Seers."

The Divinity speaking to Ioannes is one of the septenary group who poured out the libations in the final ordeal and forbids the Seer to worship him, declaring himself to be but a fellow-servitor. Then he announces himself as both the First and the Second Logos; and, lastly, calls himself Iesous, the incarnated Self of David.

The Initiate has thus "gathered himself together," unifying his whole nature, and correlating his consciousness in the four worlds.

Ch. 22: 17-21

Both the Breath and the Bride are saying "Come!" Let him who hears say "Come!" Let him who is athirst come; and let him who is willing receive the Water of Life as a free gift.

I give corroborative evidence to all who hear the arcane doctrines of the teaching of this scroll, (and I give warning) that if any one shall add (forgeries) to them, the God will add to him the scourges written in this scroll; and if any one shall erase (any portion) from the arcane doctrines of the scroll of this teaching, the God will erase his portion from the scroll of life from the Holy City, (even from) the (initiations) which are described in this scroll.

He who gives evidence of these (arcane doctrines) says:

"Verily, I am coming speedily."

Amen. Come, Master Iesous!

The Grace of the Master Iesous be with the devotees. Amen.

INTERPRETATION

In the days when books could be published only in the form of written manuscripts, it was comparatively easy for unscrupulous persons to alter them to suit their own views by expunging words and passages and by interpolating forgeries.

Religious sectaries were particularly addicted to this form of literary vandalism, as is so clearly evident from the mutilated text of portions of the New Testament, especially the epistles of Pol (Apollonius).

The statement that terrible consequences would come to any one tampering with the text of this scroll has doubtless stayed the hand of many a superstitious bigot and served to preserve it intact; but it did not frighten the clever priest who prepared the copy that became the authorized version.

But the warnings are more than a mere idle threat, for the man who would maliciously mutilate this manual, written for the higher guidance of the "little children" of the Logos, would find a grave indictment charged against him when he came to be "judged according to his works."

However, the clever priest did not mutilate the text of the Hindu Scroll. He simply made his copy of it so that it would serve the interest of the church.

That the text of the scroll has been preserved with remarkable purity is shown by the fact that the puzzles it contain have not been touched, though even slight changes by a meddlesome "redactor" might have ruined them.

Even as the Light of the Logos keeps saying to mankind, "Come," so the learner who hears that summons should repeat the call, tendering as a free gift the Water of Life to all who really thirst for it and are willing to live in such way as to be worthy to receive it.

But woe unto those who, by attempting to trade in the things of Life, have lost the Key of the Gnosis, leaving themselves locked out and hindering those who were ready to enter.

Now, the Master Iesous is the Solar Man, which alone can give absolute proof of the truth of Life Eternal. And he indeed comes swiftly to those who make themselves ready and pure and become worthy to utter the word of power-- the AMEN.

Descartes

CHAPTER NO. 37

Analysis of the Apocalypse

Down thru the years the best brains of the Christian world, warped and distorted by the teachings of the church, have tried to analyze the Apocalypse. One of these leading lights was Prof. Roswell D. Hitchcock, D.D., LL.D. In his *Analysis of the Bible*, published in 1886, of the Apocalypse, he wrote:

"1. Chapters I-III: 'Things which are,' or the then present condition of the churches. This portion, besides an account of the manner in which the writer has commissioned to write, contains seven separate addresses of epistles, to the seven principal churches of Asia, which distribute warnings, reproofs, and praises, as is deserved.

"2. Chapters IV-XIX: 'Things which shall be,' or a prophetic view of future ages. It is this later portion of the Revelations that has given rise to such an infinite number of variety of interpretations."

The Apocalypse does treat of "things which are," and of "things which shall be"; but these things refer to man and his state of consciousness and not to the conduct of churches nor to "future ages."

Emanuel Swedenberg, a prominent Christian and Mystic, wrote in Latin a book of 1200 pages, published in 1874, in which he attempted to interpret the Apocalypse; and in the confusion which he found himself, he said:

"Every one can see that the Apocalypse can by no means be explained but by the Lord alone; for each word therein contains arcana which would in no wise be known without a particular enlightenment and thus revelation: on which account it has pleased the Lord to open the sight of my (Swedenborg's) spirit and to teach me.

"Do not believe, therefore, that I have taken anything herein from myself nor from my angel, but from the Lord alone. The Lord also said to John through the angel, 'Seal not the words of the prophecy of this Book' (Chap. 22:10), by which it means that they are to be made manifest."

Swedenborg said that it had "pleased the Lord to open the sight of my spirit and to teach me" the arcane science contained in the Apocalypse; but from what he wrote of the message contained in the Apocalypse, it seems that "the Lord" knew no more about the hidden meaning of that message than did Swedenborg himself.

Swedenborg's work only increased the confusion. He viewed the book in the wrong light. He believed that it treated of "heaven and the church."

The Master who translated the Hindu Scroll into the language of his native country knew of synagogs but had never heard the word "church"; and he knew that "heaven" is a state of the Mind and not a region in space and said so (Rom 14:17).

It is true that each word in the Apocalypse contains arcana which would in no wise be known without a particular enlightenment, but that enlightenment would appertain to man's knowledge of the human body and its organs and functions.

For all the great religions of antiquity were based on the functions of the Temple not made with hands (2 Cor. 5:1).

It was not without reason that the Ancient Masters placed over the temple gate the immortal motto:

"MAN KNOW THY SELF."

Summary of the Hindu Scroll

The Scroll deals with the human body and its electric battery with seven cells, also called seals and chakras.

Asia, home land of Apollonius, represents the body; and the seven cities of Asia represent the seven cells.

The gist of the Scroll treats of the stimulation and activation of the seven cells by the Creative Fire, in its ascension (ascension of Christ) from the creative glands at the base of the spine grave to the extra-sensory glands in the brain (heaven).

The ascension of the Creative Fire up the spinal column is traced three times in the fable.

In the first of these, there is given a general description of the area of the body affected by the activation of the cell controlling that area.

In the second, there is given a brief account of the effect of the increased action in each of the seven areas, as they are stimulated by the ascension of the Creative Fire.

In the third, there is presented, in the form of Seven Scourges, the deeper effects of the increased action in each part of the body, as the ascending Fire affects and activates the seven battery cells.

The final and greatest effect in the cosmic process is the activation by the Creative Fire of the Pituitary and Pineal glands in the brain, the organs of the sixth and seventh sense powers--the powers of Seership.

CHAPTER NO. 38

Explanatory Statements

According to ancient tradition and recorded in all the great religious systems of the ancient world, so completely destroyed by the Roman Emperors from Constantine down, the terrestrial order of solarical development is but a department of that of the solar system of the universe, which is again said to be a department of a much vaster order centered in Sirius, which again may not be the ultimate.

According to Plutarch, there are two deaths--the first or physical and the second or psychical. And these occur in a sphere of existence so alien to that of our gross physical manifestation that even a description of them as occurring "after" bodily death must be interpreted in a quasi-allegorical fashion.

The transition of an entity from the material toward a solarical state involves its transfer from a continuum in which spatial attributes predominate to one in which temporal attributes increasingly secure control; until, beyond that sphere symbolized by the sub-lunar region, in the course of Solar Man's journey from the "moon" to the "sun," the medium of existence becomes time-like to the almost complete annihilation of that discrete externalism which we associate with space.

Physical death, as we observe it from without, is but one phase of a complex inward and invisible process of withdrawal.

The inner body, commonly called the etheric body, pertains rather to the outposts of the physical than to the psychic realm, constituting during physical life a connecting link between the higher and lower spheres of the microcosm.

During the moribund state of the gross body, the faculties of speech, action, sense, and the specific vital powers are gradually indrawn to their common source and center. This occurs in two steps, viz., (1) from the gross to the etheric body, and (2) from the etheric to the solaric body.

During the first step, the etheric body becomes loosened and ultimately detached from the physical, the ease and rate of this extrication depending largely on the age or previous health of the individual.

During the second step, which is really the culmination of what Plutarch termed "the first death," the psycho-vital potentialities withdrawn from the gross to the etheric body, plus those properly inherent in the latter, are similarly absorbed by the subtle desire body, which, in its turn as a result of this absorption, becomes loosened from and ultimately abandoned by the etheric body.

Thus the golden thread of Life which extended from the solarical monad above to the physical body below has, in the course of dissolution, been indrawn from the physical, thru the etheric, into the subtle body, carrying with it the potentialities of physical and ethical formal manifestation and re-integrating them with their psychic source in the vital, sensorial, and mental principles of the subtle body.

The intimacy of the union, during corporeal existence, between the body and "soul," is a common-place of popular psychology; so much so that one often encounters assertions of their virtual identity. They are not only distinguishable but separable; *and it is precisely in their separation that the process termed physical death really consists.*

It is regrettable that the process is fraught with momentous advantages to the soul-entity concerned, a fact that has always been taken most serious account of by religious systems for the sake of profit and power.

The experience of the solarical body's extricating itself from the physical body has been described by one who recovered from a death-like swoon as similar to struggling thru a dark, narrow tunnel into brilliantly-lighted and unlimited space. In a word, the solarical body withdraws itself from the physical into an individual luminous essence.

It is not uncommon for the dying person to state that he sees standing near one or more of those dearest to him who have previously died. The statement is usually made quite calmly, almost casually: "Why there is so-and-so," --wife, husband, sister, brother, son, daughter, as the case may be, without apparent realization that there is anything supernormal in the visitation.

The Second Death

The process of "the second death," involving the gradual extrication of the solar body from its disincarnate subtle vehicle, in preparation for its transference from the psychic (lunar) to the noetic or intellectual (solar) sphere, is the mystery referred to by Plutarch as the reduction of two into one.

It is not a mere reduction: as in the case of the previous physical death, the outworn vehicle is not discarded until the root-principles of its manifestation and the fruits of its experience have been indrawn, the former thus being available in the event of subsequent incarnations, the latter to be assimilated as increments of actualized faculty, wisdom, and virtue.

According to Plutarch, the second death occurs "on the moon," the dominion of Persephone, whose consort is the heavenly Hermes; and Persephone, aided by her celestial spouse, "gently and slowly separates the intellect from the "soul," --that is, from the subtle vehicle, not from the individual entity itself--a process leading to and culminating in the "second death," whereby the purified and intellectualized Solar Body is released for its journey back to the "Sun," its primal source.

The final achievement of this transition involves, according to S'ankara, the attainment of three grades of transcendence of natural and human limitations:

1. Child-like simplicity;
2. Knowledge qualifying for instruction; and
3. Solitude, in the sense of complete and final liberation.

Guenon indicates that these three attributes are implied in what is, in Vedantic terminology, called Divinity, that is, participation in the essence of Is'wara, corresponding to shaktis (feminine or power aspect) of the Hindu Trimurti--harmony, wisdom, and strength.

Behind these theosophical accounts of solar-journeys from the earth to "the moon" and thence to "the sun," lies a far more ancient fold-tradition, to the effect that man's original dwelling was "in the sun," whence he "fell," with a loss of his divine prerogative, *first* to the moon and *thence* to the earth. These are the two "falls."

According to the Upanishads, the "spiritual ascent to those higher, and even on to the highest grades of consciousness," symbolized respectively by "moon" and "sun," are not necessarily preconditions even by what Plutarch terms the first (physical) death.

We are told that there is no limit to the degree of illumination, transmutation, or liberation which is theoretically attainable during incarnation on the earth.

CHAPTER NO. 39

Seven Grades of Being

Of the seven grades of Being represented in the human microcosm, the four lower, technically denominated the "quaternary," viz., (1) physical body, (2) eidolon or aitheric double, (3) subtle or astral vehicle (supposed to be the seat of the emotions), and (4) lower manas or concrete mentality, pertain to the phenomenal order, while the three upper ones, the "ternary" or "triad," viz., (a) higher manas or abstract intellect, (b) buddhi or intuition, and (c) atma or pure ego, are noumenal and immortal.

In this super-phenomenal triad, atma-buddhi-(higher) manas, which is symbolized in many ancient religions by the Sun; and the journey to the sun is therefore nothing more nor less than a symbolic designation of the process of rendering fully actual the latent potentialities of these three transcendent microcosmic principles.

Similarly, the journey to the moon designates the much less arduous attainment of the highest grade of merely natural evolution, so far at least as human and earthly denizens of the solar system are concerned.

These two goals, "sun" and "moon," correspond respectively to the King's and Queen's Chambers of the Great Pyramid of Gizeh.

When they are both attained during physical life, it is, according to Blavatsky, the result of the concomitant activation of the two cerebral organs called the Pineal gland, which Descartes identified as the "point of contact between brain and soul," and the Pituitary gland, called the Bride of the Lamb in the Bible.

The Golden Fire

The element of Fire controls to a certain degree both the vegetal and animal kingdoms and is the only element which can subjugate the metals. Hence, from the earliest times man has venerated the element of Fire above all others.

The Creative Fire of Man originates at the base of the spinal column, which may be divided horizontally into three sections. The lowest includes the lumbar vertebrae, together with the segments forming the sacrum and coccyx.

This area is surrounded by a brick-red haze of a lurid and angry color. The haze is oily in texture and causes the sacrum and coccyx to appear the color of dried blood.

Higher up, the color is somewhat lighter and less angry looking; and still higher, the color becomes orange; and thru the sections of the back-bone composed of the twelve dorsal vertebrae, there is a golden glow radiating from a thread-like line of what appears as a river of Golden Fire. This is the Golden Oil mentioned in the Bible (Zech. 4:12).

Still higher the gold fades to yellow and becomes tinged with green, and thru the cervical (neck) section, the oil becomes faintly electric blue. Thru the Ida and Pingala nadis, this stream of Golden Fire flows up and down incessantly.

The farther up the fire goes, the thinner and less brilliant its hue, but the purer and more beautiful the colors, until finally they meet in a seething, molten mass in the pons of the medulla oblongata, the function of which science knows nothing.

At this point the Golden Fire begins to permeate the third ventricle of the brain and to stimulate the Pituitary gland.

Marriage of the Lamb

We have observed in considerable detail the Pituitary and Pineal glands of the brain. The former is the negative, passive, female pole; yet we have seen that it plays an important part in the development of the body and mind.

The Ancient Masters were well aware of these things, and they called the Pituitary the Builder of the Temple. In the Bible it is represented as Zerubbabel (Zech. 4:9).

The Pituitary appears as the initiator in the process of higher mental development as well, for it "raises" the candidate (Pineal gland) from its semi-dormant state.

Being of feminine polarity, the Pituitary performs true to its dignity by being the eternal temptress. Manly Hall wrote:

"In the Egyptian myth, Isis, who partakes of the nature of the Pituitary, conjured Ra (who represents the Sun and is symbolical of the Pineal) to disclose his sacred name, which he finally does. The physiologic process is worthy of detailed consideration.

"The Pituitary begins to glow very faintly (when stimulated by the rising creative fire), and little rippling rings of (electric) light flow out from around the gland and gradually fade a short distance away.

"An occult growth (stimulation) continues, according to the proper understanding of the law of occultism, the emanating rings around the gland grow stronger. They are not equally distributed. The circles are elongated on the side facing the third ventricle (of the brain) and extend out in graceful parabolas toward the Pineal gland.

"Gradually, as the current becomes more powerful, the circles approach ever closer to the slumbering eye of Shiva (Pineal), tinting the form of the Pineal gland with golden light and gently coaxing it into animation.

"Under the benign warmth and radiance of the Pituitary fire, the divine egg (Pineal) thrills and moves, and the magnificent mystery of occult unfoldment takes place" (Melchizedek and the Mystery of Fire).

Blavatsky phrases this part of the process in these words: "The arc (of light from the Pituitary) mounts upward more and more toward the Pineal, until finally the (electric) current striking it, just as when an electric current strikes some solid object, the dormant organ (Pineal) is awakened and set all aglowing with the akasic (creative) fire."

When that has been attained, the gap between the two glands has been bridged and connection established between the objective and subjective departments of Consciousness, raising man to the state of Cosmic Consciousness.

"This," Blavatsky explains, "is the psycho-physiological illustration of two organs on the physical plane which are concrete symbols of and represent respectively the metaphysical concepts called Manas and Buddhi. The latter, in order to be conscious on the earth plane, needs the more differentiated fire of Manas; but once the Sixth Sense (Manas, Pituitary) has awakened the Seventh Sense (Buddhi, Pineal), the light which radiates from it illuminates the fields of infinitude. For that space of time, Man becomes omniscient; the Past and the Future, Space and Time, disappear and become for him the "Present" (*Back to the Sun*, p. 118).

And so the great Carrel wrote: "For the clairvoyant there are no secrets," and the Bible says:

"There is nothing covered that shall not be revealed; and nothing hid that shall not be known" (Mat. 10:26).

And Dr. Charles Whitby writes: "Thus the journey to the 'moon' is equated with the consummation of psycho-mental development and the consequent psychic activation of the Pituitary gland; and thence the journey to the 'sun' with the awakening of the Pineal gland (involving noumenal illumination) and the 'sparking' process between the two organs with the Hermetic Marriage of the Sun (Pineal) and Moon (Pituitary), of Hermes and Aphrodite, of Ra and Isis, and, in the Apocalypse, 'the marriage of the Lamb.'" (*Back to The Sun*, p. 119).

As to the Pineal gland, Santee said: "The function of the Pineal is unknown. Descartes facetiously suggests that it is the abode of the spirit of man."

If the Pineal gland is "the abode of the spirit of man," then it represents man, for his body is only a garment in which the spirit (Solar Man) is clad.

Hall says that "the Pineal gland is the link between the consciousness of man and the invisible worlds of Nature. Whenever the arc (of electric light) of the Pituitary contacts this gland, there are flashes of temporary clairvoyance; but the process of making these two (glands) work together constantly is one requiring not only years, but lives of consecration and special physiological and biological training."

That was the great work of the Ancient Masters; and from their scriptures, devoted to that subject, has come the mass of literature contained in the Bible and distorted by the church to make it appear that the writings treat of God, Jesus, and heaven.

Hall further says that "as man's contact with the physical world grew more complete, he lost his inner understanding together with the conscious connection with the creative hierarchies. In order to regain this (conscious) connection, it is necessary for him to rise above the limitations of the physical world."

All of which is very true; but all organized institutions on earth are determined to see that man shall not rise above the limitations of the physical world, and woe unto him who seeks to interfere with that fixed standard and program.

CHAPTER NO. 40

THE COSMIC CYCLE

Life neither begins nor ends. Life is not born, and Life does not die.

"Birth and Death are but words, and both are but the surface aspects of the Inner Being." (Bhagavad Gita, p. 26).

With this ancient philosophy, the Bible fully agrees:

"Behold, I show you a mystery: We shall not sleep (in death), but we shall all be changed (to our former state of existence) in a moment, in the twinkling of an eye" (1 Cor. 15:51, 52).

For our light affliction (called death), which is but for a moment (in duration), worketh for us a far more exceeding and eternal weight of glory.

For we know what when our earthly house (physical body) is dissolved, we have a building (solar body) not made with hands, eternal in the heavens (2 Cor. 4:17; 5:1).

What is Life? For that burning question science has no definite answer.

Life is that Solar (Soul) Spark which emanates from the Sun and animates, quickens, and energizes the body, making the body what advanced scientists term an electrical machine--a machine operated by electric power.

The body, a mass of blood, bone, and flesh, is constituted of billions upon billions of electrized and intelligized solar atoms, or, more specifically, of liquefied and solidified Solar (Soul) Quintessence, which, at death, disolves into the original elements and returns to the Cosmic Reservoir.

The principal objective of initiation in the Ancient Mysteries, that great school of Arcane Science, was to teach the "man of darkness" what he actually is and explain to him that his return to his Primal Glory of Solarical Existence comes thru the creative course of discarding his physical robe in the cosmic process called Death, which is fully as much of a creative process as is that of being born in the flesh.

Only ignorance and false teaching conceal the fact that Death is just as much of a Creative Process as Birth is. For both processes are ruled by cosmic law, and both are the same in that they are creative processes.

All cosmic processes have creative propensities as their ultimate purpose. The dissolution of an animal corpse, or the disintegration of a sycamore log, is a creative process ruled by law, in which the substance of the body and the log is dissolved back into the original elements, returned to the cosmic reservoir, and thus made available for further use in the creation of more bodies and more trees.

That Creative Process is called the Cosmic Cycle. That is the Cosmic Process which LIBERATES Solar Man from his Prison of Flesh.

Birth is the cosmic process that incarcerates Solar Man in a physical body, and Death is the cosmic process that liberates Solar Man from his prison of flesh.

As the creative process termed birth produces Solar Man in the flesh, he comes clad in a covering which matches his material environment; and that material garment Solar Man sheds in the creative process called Death; and thus he is "Born Again" (Jn. 3:3, 5, 7) out of the flesh and appears robed in invisible raiment which fits him for his high state of Solaricalism--eternal Solar (Soul) Existence.

When the basic facts of creative processes are properly presented, we realize that the Real Man is a Son of the Sun and is not mysteriously made by a mythical God invented by the church to deceive men and enslave the masses.

In spite of the illusion of visible appearance and false knowledge, Solar Man remains the same and changes not as to his Inner Self, even while dwelling on earth in a form of flesh. It is his external garment only and not his Internal Being, which changes.

It is axiomatic that something cannot come from nothing, regardless of what the church says or what it made its God say.

Solar Man could not appear as a visible figure in the material world if he did not first exist in the invisible world before he is born in the flesh.

Correctly understood, Birth and Death are definite processes in the Cosmic Cycle. Birth brings Solar Man into the visible world, while Death takes him out of it; and he then exists in the invisible world the same after Death as he did before Birth.

The Solar Cycle illustrates the Life Cycle. The Sun, setting on the one side, rises on the other. Every moment of its motion is a setting at one point and a rising at another.

As the Sun rises in its setting and sets in its rising, so Solar Man sets (dies) in the invisible realm as he rises (is born) in the visible realm; and he is born (rises) again in the invisible realm as he dies (sets) in the physical realm.

Birth and Death, Sunrise and Sunset, are the products of illusions, thoughts, dreams, and the fears of the Fool.

Creation is ruled by the Law of the Cosmic Cycle. Visible forms are produced from invisible elements, and visible forms are reduced to invisible elements.

Created objects exist in a state of change; nothing begins; nothing ends; and the primal pattern, the core at the center, remains permanent and changeless.

Man is a creature of the Cosmic Cycle, going thru definite changes as to his material garment but at the core remaining always the same entity. The internal core, the pattern, the solar body, changes not. That is the Real Being.

However, it is well that man in the flesh is in darkness as to his Real Self while dwelling on the earth; for he would otherwise have little incentive or inclination to go on and suffer the burdens and hardships of earthly life.

And so, it is a wise provision of Cosmic Creation that closes the human Mind and blacks out Reality so that the Mind cannot definitely envision the glorious world of its origin.

But ten thousand years ago, the Masters discovered that it is possible to pierce the "wall of darkness" and penetrate into the glorious light of Solarical Immortality, on the other side of the black river.

This top secret of the Masters is symbolized in the Bible as "a door opened in heaven" (Rev. 4:1).

Thru that "door" or "window in space", man can see the physical, etherical, and astral worlds.

Of this ancient secret Bailey wrote: "The Jewel or diamond concealed in the egoic lotus is the window of the Monad whereby he looks outward into the three worlds. The third eye (Pineal gland of the brain) is the window of the Ego functioning on the physical plane whereby he looks inward into the three worlds." (*Cosmic Fire*, p. 1130).

This great secret was always heavily veiled in all ancient scriptures to conceal it from the masses. It is the chief topic of the Bible and yet unknown to the multitude and to the clergy.

The Masters realized that the process by which this may be accomplished should be kept carefully guarded from all but the initiates, in order that the common man would remain in darkness as to his Real Self and be satisfied to live out his allotted time on earth.

For if the masses knew the secret of the Cosmic Cycle, many would not choose to go on and endure the so-called blessings and pleasures of earthly life, where tyrants and despots rule the land with an iron rod, even under the best systems of government that wise men have been able to devise.

And we should not shun nor avoid the glaring fact that much of the misery of the masses is also due to the deceitful and deliberate work of the church.

The church has very cleverly presented a revolting picture of life and a worse one of death and the hereafter, all of which cause man to dwell between two dreaded conditions while he lives on earth.

The church teaches man to spend his days thanking a mythical God for the "mercies and blessings" he receives on earth and to depend on the church for the help that it claims to be able to give him in making "peace" with that Tyrannical Monster of Vengeance (Deut. 32:35; Ps. 91:1), in order that his "Soul," after death, shall not suffer eternal torment in a lake of fire.

He who discovers the secret of the Cosmic Cycle and fails and refuses to live on that low level of darkness created by the church does so at the risk of grave peril and endless persecution.

It is almost unbelievable to realize that the only measures of protection standing between that man and death are the laws of this country which were enacted purposely and expressly to check the ruthless course of the church, which boldly declares, thru the voice of its brazen leaders, that the death penalty is essential to secure the aims of the church.

Pope Leo XIII approved a Book of Canon Law in which it is said:

"The death sentence is a necessary and efficacious means for the Church to attain its ends." (*Progressive World*, March-1956, p. 54).

In that monumental work titled "History of the Inquisition," are told the terrible tales of the secret transactions of those horrific catholic tribunals which make one's blood run cold, as one learns a little of how the church authorities slaughtered millions of people during the Dark Ages for refusing to accept and receive the fraudulent Jesus as "the only begotten Son of God." (Jn. 3:16).

(THE END)

CPSIA information can be obtained
at www.ICGtesting.com
Printed in the USA
LVOW04s1357031017
551022LV00006B/229/P